God has used David Bryant in my life as a model, a brother and a fellow servant. Is God preparing His Church for a worldwide revival? *Stand in the Gap* makes a strong case for such a visitation. I couldn't put this book down. From de within me welled up a fresh hope, a renewed confid and great joy. Clear the decks, grab the book a out how you can stand in the gap

JOE ALDRICH

President, Multnomah Bible
Portland, Oregon

David Bryant understands the times. And he understands prayer. These merge in *Stand in the Gap* to produce a vital, timely and fresh book that will challenge you to help shape history—God's way!

JOHN D. BECKETT

Chairman of the Board, Intercessors for America
Elyria, Ohio

Jesus said, "Open your eyes and look at the fields! They are ripe for the harvest" (John 4:35). *Stand in the Gap* gives us a fresh look at the harvest fields of our day. Those who want to have a part in the worldwide movement of God need to read this book.

LEE BRASE

Beaverton, Oregon

David Bryant is a major voice for prayer and revival in the Church today, and this book is a major message which can help set the Church afire. WARNING: This book may change your life...and our world.

BILL BRIGHT
Founder and President, Campus Crusade for Christ International
Orlando, Florida

David Bryant's *Stand in the Gap* gives us all fresh perspective on the recent decade of prayer efforts around the world. Rejoice in the widening panorama and renewed promise in prayer, and look for even greater victories through prayer in future years.

BOBBYE BYERLY
U.S. National President, Aglow International
Lynnwood, Washington

Every committed Christian will be both challenged and helped by this remarkable and powerful book by one of God's choice servants.

PAUL A. CEDAR
Chairman, Mission America
Minneapolis, Minnesota

After 47 years of earnestly praying for revival, I am still asking, "Will it ever come? What will it take to see it happen?" David Bryant tackles these questions and more in his timely book. As you read *Stand in the Gap*, you will be called— called to stand with Jesus for the world!

EVELYN CHRISTENSON
Chair, AD 2000 North America Women's Track
President, United Prayer Ministry
St. Paul, Minnesota

In *Stand in the Gap*, David Bryant gives us the gift of hope. Full of instructive stories and practical steps, this sweeping overview of revival movements lifts the reader from lethargy to energy and vision.

JOHN DAWSON
Founder, International Reconciliation Coalition
Sunland, California

Stand in the Gap will help you take a quantum leap toward getting in step with God's end-time purposes for His Church and taking your part in the worldwide revival. David Bryant's message is urgent, compelling and convincing.

JOY DAWSON
International Bible teacher and author
Tujunga, California

Christ is calling His Church to the front lines of practical involvement "in the gap" on behalf of our neighbors, cities and the nations of the world. David Bryant's *Stand in the Gap* is an all-time, classic mission manifesto on how to pursue our rightful role in the coming worldwide spiritual awakening.

DICK EASTMAN
President, Every Home for Christ
Colorado Springs, Colorado

Are you hesitant to "stand in the gap"? Bryant sheds light on what the gap is and how God will transform us in order to fill it. *Stand in the Gap* shows us how our daily obedience fits into God's bigger picture of what He wants to do in our world. We all need to ponder the message of this book.

PAUL FLEISCHMANN
Executive Director, National Network of Youth Ministries
San Diego, California

No man is more devoted to standing in the gap for our nation than David Bryant. This is a faith-reviving book, stirring us to believe that God will revive the Church and save our country. This is must-reading for those who love the Lord and our great land.

E. BRANDT GUSTAVSON

President, National Religious Broadcasters
Manassas, Virginia

Stand in the Gap will cause you to see the world the way God sees it, through the eyes of hope. This inspiring book presents clear, proven strategies for making our lives count for Christ in our churches, communities and world. I highly recommend this book for anyone who wants to be in the flow of what the Holy Spirit is doing right now.

TED HAGGARD

Pastor, New Life Church
Colorado Springs, Colorado

Filled with pertinent information on the worldwide prayer movement of the past decade, *Stand in the Gap* provides a timely wake-up call for readers of the previous edition of David Bryant's book. This new edition combines sound, biblical principles regarding prayer and evangelism with practical application. Those who *haven't* read the first edition are in for an exciting journey of discovering how God would use them to impact their world.

JANE HANSEN

International President, Aglow International
Lynnwood, Washington

Stand in the Gap will be a catalyst for the follower of Christ who wants to join the Lord in what He is doing in the world. David Bryant will inform, challenge, instruct, inspire and motivate you to be a carrier of the hope in Christ to our world—starting right where you are. Read it and catch the vision!

Ray Hoo

Vice President, The U.S. Navigators
Colorado Springs, Colorado

Exciting information documenting how God is at work as never before in history blends with practical suggestions on how each of us can be a vital part of the coming great awakening. I strongly recommend *Stand in the Gap*.

Larry L. Lewis

National Facilitator, Celebrate Jesus 2000
Lilburn, Georgia

David Bryant lays one of the foundation stones for a renewed vision of world evangelization. This updated work provides us a structure upon which a more functional, beautiful representation of God's Kingdom community can be built. A wonderful, inspired mixture of the practical and visionary.

Paul E. McKaughan

President & CEO, Evangelical Fellowship of Mission Agencies
Washington, D.C.

Stand in the Gap is must-reading for every Christian who shares David Bryant's unshakable, hope-filled conviction that we are on the threshold of the greatest revival in the history of the Church. Let's prayerfully stand in the gap together, release all pea-sized views of Christianity and join feeder streams leading to an authentic, world-sized revival!

Stephen A. Macchia

President, Evangelistic Association of New England
Burlington, Massachusetts

David Bryant is a gift to the Church. He sees what many do not see. Several years ago, *In the Gap* was a "jump start" for me, leading me to a new level of missions understanding. David has fully updated his classic book with current missiological facts, an inspiring update on the worldwide prayer movement and hopeful signs of a coming global revival and harvest of souls "from every nation, tribe and language." Get ready for this great outpouring of the Holy Spirit with David Bryant's practical study guide and plan for personal action. I suggest you purchase the book in quantities and give it to promising young people and leaders in your church.

BOB RICKER

President, Baptist General Conference
Arlington, Illinois

Stand in the Gap will add fuel to the fire of awakening. With its timely message on prayer and hope and a stirring call to action, I plan to use the book with youth leaders and student leaders.

BARRY ST. CLAIR

Executive Director, Reach Out Ministries
Norcross, Georgia

Without sweeping revival, our cities will continue to stumble toward chaos, our families will collapse and relativism will complete its destruction of our culture. David Bryant offers hope because he believes God is sending revival. We need to hear his ringing call for Christians who will plead with God for worldwide revival and follow his concrete suggestions for action.

RONALD J. SIDER

President, Eastern Baptist Theological Seminary
Wynnewood, Pennsylvania

Stand in the Gap is a must-read book for all who long for and pray for revival. God's grace will be powerfully released, and many lives will be touched if intercessors take this book seriously.

ALVIN J. VANDER GRIEND

Director, Houses of Prayer Everywhere
Grand Rapids, Michigan

Stand in the Gap is a must-read for every person who desires to reach the people in his area for Christ, and who is determined to make a difference in his community. I recommend this book to all serious Christians.

THOMAS WANG

President, Great Commission Center
Argyle, Texas

Almighty God continues today to look for people willing to "give it up" and stand in the gap for Him. I believe that anyone who accepts this challenge must begin on his face in prayer. If there is any value in having a modern-day guide that will lead you to this broken, yet honorable place before God, read this book. David will lead you there.

RALEIGH B. WASHINGTON

Vice President for Reconciliation, Promise Keepers
Pastor, The Rock Church
Chicago, Illinois

A God-inspired and timely gift to Christians seeking new depth and dimension in prayer, evangelism and discipling. I enthusiastically endorse this volume as an indispensable "manual for mission."

COMMISSIONER ROBERT A. WATSON

National Commander, The Salvation Army
Alexandria, Virginia

STAND IN THE GAP

HOW TO GET READY FOR THE COMING WORLD REVIVAL

David Bryant

Regal

A Division of Gospel Light
Ventura, California, U.S.A.

Published by Regal Books
A Division of Gospel Light
Ventura, California, U.S.A.
Printed in U.S.A.

Regal Books is a ministry of Gospel Light, an evangelical Christian publisher dedicated to serving the local church. We believe God's vision for Gospel Light is to provide church leaders with biblical, user-friendly materials that will help them evangelize, disciple and minister to children, youth and families.

It is our prayer that this Regal book will help you discover biblical truth for your own life and help you meet the needs of others. May God richly bless you.

For a free catalog of resources from Regal Books/Gospel Light please contact your Christian supplier or call 1-800-4-GOSPEL.

Cover Design by Barbara Levan Fisher
Interior Design by Britt Rocchio
Edited by Karen Kaufman

Library of Congress Cataloging-in-Publication Data
Bryant, David, 1945-
    Stand in the gap : how to get ready for the coming world revival / David Bryant.
    p.   cm.
    Rev. ed. of: In the gap. 1984.
    Includes bibliographical references.
    ISBN 0-8307-1936-9 (trade paper)
    1. Missions. 2. Revivals. 3. Evangelistic work. 4. Church renewal. 5. Christianity—Forecasting.
I. Bryant, David, 1945-
    In the gap. II. Title.
    BV2063.B74   1997   97-19964
    266'.001—dc21   CIP

1 2 3 4 5 6 7 8 9 10 11 12 13 14 15 16 / 04 03 02 01 00 99 98 97

Rights for publishing this book in other languages are contracted by Gospel Literature International
(GLINT). GLINT also provides technical help for the adaptation, translation and publishing of Bible
study resources and books in scores of languages worldwide. For further information, contact
GLINT, P.O. Box 4060, Ontario, CA 91761-1003, U.S.A., or the publisher.

To Robyne,
my precious wife
and strong companion,
who serves with me
as one...in the Gap.

— *R o m a n s   1 5 : 6*

CONTENTS

■

PART I
IN THE GAP

PART II
GET READY FOR THE COMING WORLD REVIVAL

FOREWORD

⁚

As a coach, I would be pleased whenever I'd see one of my football players perched on a bench memorizing plays—the nuts and bolts of who does what, where and when. But if I ever ran across a player who only focused on the play diagrams, I knew he'd never be a great player. He not only needed to know the specific plays, but he also had to understand the game.

David Bryant's book *Stand in the Gap* is all about understanding the game, the big picture of what God is doing and how we fit in. In the Promise Keepers' movement, we men challenge each other to seven specific promises—the "plays" we need to know as growing disciples of Jesus Christ.

We all know that even fulfilling these promises won't make us great men of God. We also need to understand the big picture of what God is doing, to understand our point in history.

Keeping the promises, running the plays isn't enough. But we can take those disciplines and step into position in the awesome move of God unfolding across our nation and across the planet. We live in a day of great hope—the hope of a genuine, biblical revival. You and I are meant to be a part of it.

David is calling for all of us to pray for and prepare for a God-given spiritual awakening to Christ. He's done it for years. No one does it better. It's the call of Ezekiel 22:30, and millions of men and women are rising up. Join David, me and all of us shoulder-to-shoulder to stand in the Gap.

Coach Bill McCartney
Founder, Promise Keepers

Acknowledgments

⊞

This volume is more than simply a major revision of a former publication. It also represents nearly 20 years (since *In the Gap* was first available) of schooling for me at the feet of some of the Church's greatest statesmen and missiologists. My indebtedness to them is incalculable.

I also want to thank the Board of Directors, my ministry team (scattered between Chicago and New York offices), our National Board of Advocates and a multitude of intercessors and supporters—all dedicated to the surviving and thriving of Concerts of Prayer International. If it were not for them I may never have had the courage to remain "standing in the Gap." But because they have stood with me, we have seen God do great and mighty things throughout the years, filling us with unquenchable hope about a coming national and world revival in our generation.

The greatest team of all, however, has been my family. As it was in 1979, this substantially revised *In the Gap* is once again dedicated to my precious wife, Robyne. In so many ways, this book comes out of *both* of our hearts. To Adam, Bethany and Benjamin, I simply want to say: "Thank you for your growing faithfulness and personal pursuit of the vision explored in this book. We walk together in the Gap."

Special thanks to Bill Greig Jr. (a member of the COPI Board); also Bill Greig III and Kyle Duncan at Gospel Light/Regal Books. You took some bold steps to republish (and revise) a book that has been around for 20 years. I am grateful for your confidence—most of all, in God.

And to Bill Stearns, president of World Christian Inc., and master wordsmith: My glowing appreciation for your capable counsel throughout the metamorphosising of *In the Gap*. I could not have done it without you. Incidentally, great job on the Study Guide at the back!

Together with all of these people, I offer this book up to my Lord, Jesus Christ—the One who will ultimately *fill* the Gap with Himself.

Introduction

FROM ONE EGG TO ANOTHER

::

It may be hard for an egg to turn into a bird: it would be
a jolly sight harder for it to learn to fly while remaining
an egg. We are like eggs at present. And you cannot go
on indefinitely being just an ordinary, decent egg.
We must be hatched or go bad.[1]

—C.S. Lewis

Lewis is right. Hatch we must! The question is: How? One answer is
given in this book: Get out of your shells and get into the "gap." In a
sense, believers who are moving out to embrace the hope of revival
have already become hatching eggs. I think Lewis would be satisfied.

To say that *Stand in the Gap* hatches restless eggs, however, isn't
book-intro hype, because the impact of this book lies not in its liter-
ary genius but in its focus. It zeroes in on what God is doing and how
we can be part of it.

God is doing wonderful works of revival among the children of men
(as the chorus goes in Psalm 107), and it's exciting to be invited to participate with Him. Some of these wonderful works have to do with His
shaking up the American Church, readying us for possibly the greatest
revival in our history. I've seen this unfolding firsthand, for example:
speaking to hundreds of thousands of Promise Keepers in stadiums
across the country.

But, of course, His plan for our day doesn't end with us; Americans are only 6 percent of the world's population. Our God is a global God with a heart for every people. His is a plan that Christ will fulfill among all the nations. And the coming revival is exclusively about that plan—even as it touches your life.

God is cracking shells these days by the millions worldwide. Yours may be one. You can expect new life—revival—to spring forth—for you, your family, your church, your community and beyond. But revival doesn't happen by reading a book.

THE FOUNDATIONS

Knowing that God is up to something significant and wishing to be part of it isn't enough, of course. He always works from a foundation.

On an individual level, that foundation is personal salvation in Jesus Christ. If you haven't been, as the old gospel song puts it, "washed in the blood of the Lamb," this in-the-Gap business isn't for you. Yet. (See Resources for some clear help about how you can come to know salvation in Christ.)

On a corporate level, God always works in the life of a believer or a congregation according to what He has already revealed in His Word, the Bible. No amount of cheerleading or how-to chapters are going to prepare a local fellowship for the coming national and global revival unless the people of that fellowship are obedient to the Word.

But that's why *Stand in the Gap* will "work" in your life. I'm going to presume you know Jesus Christ, and I'm going to presume you are linked with other Christians who are restless enough—with shells cracking here and there—to flat out obey what God says. I'm going to expect that you are feeling you've got to hatch—or go bad!

TESTED PRINCIPLES

Would you love to end each day by putting your head on your pillow and confidently saying, "I know this day my life has counted strategically toward a God-given awakening to Christ in my church, in my commmunity and in my world"? In other words, wouldn't you like to daily live filled with an "abounding hope in the power of the Holy

Spirit" (see Rom. 15:13, *NKJV*)? Especially the hope of revival? You'd be hatched and ready to fly, right? Well, the bottom-line impact of the principles in this book have potential for doing just that.

Stand in the Gap is the twenty-first-century version of *In the Gap*, a book I churned out back in the late '70s. And *In the Gap* got away from me. I mean, it has showed up in the most remote places throughout the world, studied by tens of thousands of believers restless to move out, restless to hatch into who they can become in Jesus Christ. This isn't bragging. I am simply reassuring you that the basics of this tested, proven book will change your life and the lives of those you love, wherever they are found "in the Gap."

Stand in the Gap is actually a companion volume to three other books I have written. Each can add unique dimensions to complement what I have written in this book about our adventures in the Gap. Consider sometime exploring *Concerts of Prayer* (Regal), *The Hope at Hand* (Baker) and *Messengers of Hope* (Baker).

Our *Stand in the Gap* study together can hatch eggs because it is:

1. Biblical in its approach to revival and our part in it;
2. Christ-centered, with Jesus—not manmade programs—as the Lord of revival;
3. Serious about national and world evangelization;
4. Realistic...because I'm still hatching too!

Now, what is this Gap we're getting ready to stand in? Read on!

Note
1. C. S. Lewis, *Mere Christianity* (New York: Simon & Schuster, 1952), p. 169.

PART I
In the Gap

⠿

"I looked for a man among them who would build up the wall and stand before me in the gap on behalf of the land."

—*Ezekiel 22:30*

1 | THERE IS A GAP...AND YOU'RE IN IT RIGHT NOW!

FACING THE GAP—FROM TOLEDO TO TIMBUKTU

It was an extraordinary moment...one I'll remember forever. They came from more than 200 nations—some 4,000 strong—leaders at the front lines of the missionary advance worldwide. Gathered for the first time like this, these missionary leaders gathered to set in place strategic coalitions for completing Christ's global cause in this generation.

Already we had spent six days consulting, planning, researching, dreaming. The previous night we had attended a six-hour gathering of 70,000 university students in Seoul's Olympic Stadium. We beheld the breathtaking spectacle with more than 60,000 written commitments to go anywhere and do anything to make Christ known among the nations.

Now, here we were 24 hours later (at the Global Consultation on World Evangelization in Seoul, Korea, 1995), the leaders to whom these students were looking, ready to enter into our own night of prayer. Then it happened. Guiding it from the front, I also was caught by the impact of the moment. For the first time in the history of the Church, 4,000 mission activists, with thousands of years among them of standing in the Gap, poured out their hearts as one person, praying for a single overriding divine intervention for our generation.

We cried out to God for a worldwide outpouring of the Holy Spirit in genuine Christ-centered revival within every congregation so the whole Church could take the whole gospel throughout the whole world. I believe that moment was a watershed for world evangelization. How it would have thrilled the old prophet Ezekiel—the one who first highlighted the Gap for me, over which we prayed that night.

Ezekiel's book gives us a stirring glimpse into the heart of God (see Ezek. 22:30). A wall around Israel had broken down, and God was grieved at this tragedy. God could have done anything, of course; He could have fixed the wall. And yet He has chosen to implement His historic plan of redemption through human agents. Through Ezekiel, God looked for someone to be a defensive force against attackers in this emergency, to hold a sword in one hand while rebuilding the wall with the other. God was looking for someone to stand in the Gap.

What Is This Gap?

The "wall" for Israel meant protection and refuge. It also provided a focus for the nation (because it surrounded the central city) and gave definition to God's presence and reign. In that sense, the wall was the "sign" of God's favor, and good repair was a witness to other nations that God had a people on the earth—that they were His community, and that inside the wall *He could be found.*

The "gap," then, was a breakdown in all that the wall meant—in protection, in focus, in awareness of God's presence and in witness. A gap in the wall was a warning that all was not well. It was a breach that, left unattended, would surely become a foothold and entryway for enemies.

What would happen if no one stood in the Gap?

1. The breach, if allowed to remain, would guarantee God's judgment. Because the breach had actually been caused by Israel's rebellion, it would mean the desolation of the land.
2. The breach, if allowed to remain, would also mean the loss of witness before the nations. The city would be destroyed by its enemies and taken captive. Israel would no longer possess the land—the base of operations for God's kingdom at that point in redemptive history. Thus the concern was like that of the prayer in Joel: "Spare your people....Why

should they say among the peoples, 'Where is their God?'"
(Joel 2:17).

3. If allowed to remain, the breach would mean a temporary
    break, a parenthesis in the ongoing fulfillment of God's
    vision for the nation, for its future glory and for its influ-
    ence upon all the nations. In that sense, another kind of
    "gap" would exist between what God wanted to do world-
    wide and what would actually happen if His people
    remained in rebellion—if no one stood.

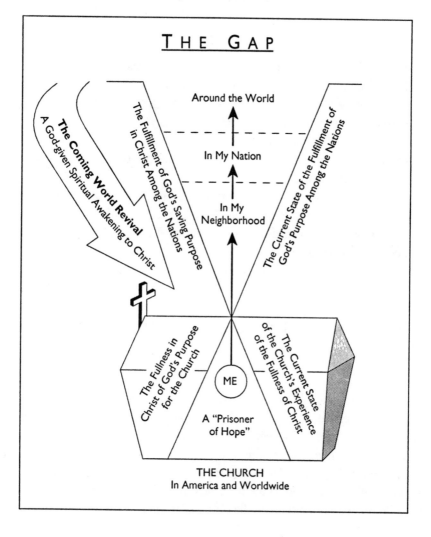

In Israel's case at that time, nobody responded. God's lament was: "But I found none" (Ezek. 22:30).

Who was to fill this "breach"? According to Ezekiel 33:7, it should have been "watchmen" who were to proclaim the purposes of God to

##

As believers we are all in the Gap. We have no choice.

##

the people of God, so they would turn and live. These servants were to be, at the same time, literally "before My face"—representing the situation before God, and representing God to the people. They were to *stand* in the Gap, to be strategically involved.

Throughout the book of Ezekiel, the ultimate bridging of the Gap is clearly not a human effort; it occurs as a result of God's divine initiative.

We call this divine initiative *revival.*

Ezekiel's vision of full-blown revival—of restoring blessing, of reaching the nations, even of rebuilding the temple—begins by describing a new *wall* (see Ezek. 40:5). Someone must stand in the Gap, to begin repairing the wall.

Actually, as believers we are all in the Gap. We have no choice. The Gap is the most significant issue facing any Christian—what it is, why it is and what a follower of Jesus must do about it. My question (and God's question in Ezekiel 22:30) is: Who will *stand* in that Gap?

FACING THE GAP

Do we even realize that a Gap exists? A Gap between who we are and what we can be in Jesus Christ? A Gap separating the Father heart of God from all the kids, men and women who don't know Him? It's a Gap that meanders out before us from wherever we live—Toledo, Ohio, or Wahoo, Nebraska—out across the world to Timbuktu (Can you find it on a globe?) and on to the uttermost parts of the earth.

Before we vow to stand in the Gap, we first need to *see* it. Paul prayed:

I pray that the eyes of your heart may be enlightened, so
that you may know what is the hope of His calling, what are
the riches of the glory of His inheritance in the saints, and
what is the surpassing greatness of His power toward us
who believe. These are in accordance with the working of
the strength of His might which He brought about in Christ,
when He raised Him from the dead, and seated Him at His
right hand in the heavenly places, far above all rule and
authority and power and dominion, and every name that is
named, not only in this age, but also in the one to come....
And gave Him as head over all things (Eph. 1:18-23, *NASB*).

Paul prays that every believer's heart will be able to see. See what?
To see the big picture, to see that we are destined and appointed to live
for "the praise of [God's] glory...according to the kind intention of His
will" (vv. 5,6). His will is a plan for "the fullness of the times, that is,
the summing up of all things in Christ, things in the heavens and things
upon the earth" (v. 10).

When the hearts of believers are able to really see, they will make
an extraordinary discovery in three important areas, and the awakening in their hearts will happen!

Paul asks God to:

1. Awaken us to the *hope* of our calling in Christ (see v. 18).
    That solid hope both now and in eternity are the victories
    awaiting those "destined" to stand in the Gap;
2. Awaken us to God's *resources* in the saints (see v. 18). We
    will sense our part in Christ's global Body and be ade-
    quately equipped to bring praise to God's grace among all
    the nations;
3. Awaken us to God's *power* at work in us (see vv. 19-23). This
    is the very power that is right now summing up all things
    under Christ as Lord and doing so through the Church
    throughout the world.

Paul carefully notes in his prayer that *only* the Holy Spirit can bring
this awakening to pass. The Spirit alone can give us new vision. Paul

prays further in Ephesians 3 that the Spirit will strengthen God's people in their inner beings with the mighty love of Christ, which, in turn, can fill the height, depth, width and length of the whole Gap through them (see vv. 14-19). Is this practical?

Believe it or not, Paul's prayers are being answered *today*:

About 70 percent of all progress toward completing the Great Commission has taken place since 1900. Of that, 70 percent has occurred since World War II. And 70 percent of that has come about since 1992.

Missionary statesman Ralph Winter says, "We have before us the brightest set of hope-filled resources, the most extensive global network of eager believers in thousands of prayer cells and strategizing committees. We have never ever had as many competent, sold-out soldiers for Jesus Christ. The job to be done is now dramatically smaller in terms of our resources than ever before."

Christians can be found in 22,000 denominational groups worldwide, each of which has special ways of reflecting Christ's grace and power before the nations.

Currently more than 7 million evangelical, Bible-believing congregations in the world are moving out across their communities, cultures and into other cultures in the name of Christ.

Five hundred million of the world's Christians have intentionally committed to help fulfill the Great Commission. This number is growing by 6.9 percent a year, which is six times faster than the population generally.

In the hands of more than 4 million full-time Christian workers, there are 44 million computers, 50 million Bibles, and billions of dollars in uncommitted tithes to support them. Money, manpower and technology are available for the cause of Christ as never before.

There are 2,520 Christian radio/TV stations throughout the world. About 4.6 billion of the world's population receive gospel radio broadcasts in their own tongues.

With the great increase of youth mission movements worldwide, we are seeing more than 200,000 believers involved in short-term missions each year.

Currently a movement of prayer among Chinese churches throughout the Chinese world has thousands praying for revival in the churches of America.

A growing search for spiritual meaning is taking place in America. *Time* calls it a "generation of seekers." So does *Newsweek* in its cover article "A Time to Seek," discussing the return to religion among baby boomers. A recent Barna Research Group survey discovered that 90 percent pray to God, 61 percent make specific requests of God, 60 percent do so every day and 46 percent listen silently for the answers. An openness for the kind of breakthrough that comes in revival is obvious.

The evangelical movement in the United States is the most organized, populous, financially prosperous, strategic thinking, visible, mobile, culturally pervasive and prolific of any genuine Christian movement in the history of the world.

A string of more than 1,000 Christian radio stations currently blankets the country and can provide a significant resource for pulling the Christian community together in a time of revival.[1]

Eddie Smith, coordinator of prayer mobilization for Mission America, notes in his *Watchmen National Prayer Alert* bulletin:

> There is an explosion of inner-city ministries across the United States. The Church is taking back the abandoned downtown areas of our cities. Interestingly, the courthouse and other seats of political power typically reside in these areas that the Church once abandoned during "white flight." Now Hispanics, blacks and whites alike are targeting the inner cities with powerful social and evangelisitc ministries.
>
> America's prison system is in spiritual renewal! It is not uncommon to visit a prison chapel and experience the same passionate, aggressive, intimate worship one would experience at a Promise Keepers men's conference. Involvement in prison Bible studies is exploding!
>
> There is a wonderful partnership taking place in the Church of Jesus Christ. An excellent example would be the Southern Baptist Convention "loaning" their Home Mission Board president to work interdenominationally to coordinate Celebrate Jesus 2000, an initiative to pray for and present the gospel to every man, woman, boy and girl in the United States before the year 2000....

I would describe most of our churches and cities in a
pre-revival state. There is prayer going up 24 hours a day.
Some city leaders have literally mapped the square miles
of their cities and assigned intercessors over each portion
of the map. Others are establishing hundreds of neighborhood houses of prayer. Others are strategically prayer-
walking their cities.[2]

Across America and the globe, God's Spirit is placing new vision in
millions of believers' hearts, a new personal awakening. You're probably reading this now because God is opening your eyes and stirring an
awakening in your heart.

Wouldn't it be wonderful if God would give everyone in your fellowship that personal sense of awakening? What if the apostle Paul's
Ephesians prayers were actually answered in your Bible study group or
your church—and in groups such as yours throughout the United States
and the whole world? Believers would be increasingly impatient with
the routines of average lives, with the mechanics of "churchianity."

So, you're ready to move out, to stand in the Gap? Great! Now, if
that's the potential in just one heart, think of what could happen within the tens of millions of believers in our country if a Great Awakening
came with full force.

I believe it will.

IT HAS HAPPENED BEFORE; IT CAN HAPPEN AGAIN

The coming awakening could well follow the pattern of the Student
Volunteer Movement from about a century ago. It began when 100 students volunteered for missionary service in 1886 at a Bible conference
led by evangelist Dwight Moody, himself a product of the Great
Awakening of 1858. The movement grew for the following 40 years,
placing 20,000 new missionaries overseas, with tens of thousands
more who volunteered as the home-front team—standing in the Gap.

As students graduated, the Movement soon impacted local churches
as well as the college campuses of America, mobilizing the vision of
laypeople through extensive study programs about world missions and
directly through the Laymen's Missions Movement. Student Volunteers

disseminated evangelistic literature and influenced Christian periodicals to feature evangelism and missions in a fresh and vital way. Many Christians were convinced that such a stupendous enterprise as world evangelization was feasible through the resources available to them.

Local churches found a new faith for reaching out in the name of Christ through their personal interactions with enthused Student Volunteers. Whole denominations were inspired to increase the efforts of their own missions boards. Giving to outreach increased sharply.

Nominal Christians were renewed and unbelievers were won to Christ as our society became aware that Christianity was a present-day, vital, worldwide, world-changing movement sufficient for the needs of people in their neighborhoods and the world. Christians were moved to aggressive evangelism at home and abroad.

Believers from different denominations found a rare sense of unity when the mission of the Church became a higher priority than the lesser things that often divide.

Can it happen again? Are Christians today looking for a cause this big, this compelling, this life changing? Or do the true believers of America even *care* about revival?

I believe that today's Christians are much like the students I ministered to back in the late '70s, who were often labeled "apathetic" when compared to the radical student activists of the early '70s. But I discovered that nonactivists are not always genuinely apathetic. They are simply, in the words of a *Time* magazine article, "a patchwork of dramatics awaiting a drama."[3]

For Christians in America today, that drama could be the revival of the American Church—a revival spilling into an earthshaking, global awakening to Jesus Christ.

Let's think through the possibilities of that Great Awakening—coming to the Gap near you!

Notes

1. David Bryant, *The Hope at Hand* (Grand Rapids: Baker Books, 1995), pp. 221-228.
2. Eddie Smith, *Watchmen National Prayer Alert*, January-February 1997, pp. 1,2,6.
3. Frank Trippet, "The '70s: A Time of Pause," *Time* magazine (December 25, 1978): 84.

2 | COMING TO THE GAP: A GREAT AWAKENING TO CHRIST

THE CONFIDENT HOPE THAT CAN REVOLUTIONIZE YOUR LIFE FOREVER

I mentioned my experience in leading a Concert of Prayer at the Global Consultation on World Evangelization in chapter 1. I want to tell you about two other meetings that occurred a year later, in February 1996. Both were equally historic.

Both took place at the Georgia Dome. At the beginning of the week, 7,500 youth pastors and workers—the largest interdenominational meeting of its kind ever held—assembled under a huge banner that read: "United for Spiritual Awakening." One proof that they meant business was a stack of commitment cards placed in the center of the arena. The cards had been signed by teenagers from across America who were vowing to be sexually pure. The stack of cards rose up into the Dome—more than 300,000 in all!

Toward the end of the week, a second conference summoned nearly 40,000 pastors—the most ever linked in one event in Church history. It too was focused primarily on the coming revival God is preparing for our nation. In fact, they embraced a written covenant to that end before leaving.

Both meetings crackled with an overwhelming sense of hope! This became especially apparent to me as I lead both meetings in a time of concerted prayer. I watched these leaders praying with an understanding of the ways of God that said to Him, essentially: "The awakening to Christ you want to pour out on our nation is so wonderful that we simply can't live without it. But, it is so wonderful we know that we will never produce it. So, our eyes are fixed on Christ, and in His name we invite You to do it." Without question, each leader left those meetings convinced that God would answer, and determined to be ready to enter in when He does.

As the president of an international ministry, I guess *I'm* expected to be such an activist. But with all the discouraging bad news to pray about in the United States and the world, some people are surprised that my activism (and that of these leaders) flows out of hope—not panic—out of anticipation more than desperation!

I stated pretty brashly in *The Hope at Hand,* a companion study volume to this book, that with unshakable conviction I believe we are on the threshold of the greatest revival in the history of the Church. I believe we can get ready to stand in the Gap—not with a martyrlike resignation, but with God-centered hope. Standing tough for Jesus Christ isn't even a matter of passively waiting for revival. It is, with eager anticipation, hastening the coming of that revival that will flood the Gaps in our churches, communities and cultures.

We can adopt the athlete's attitude before a contest—"like a strong man to run its race" (Ps. 19:5, *NKJV*). Yes, we will experience nervousness. Yes, it is not going to be easy. But a bold hope of victory will tingle in our muscles: We're going to do something tough, and we're going to win!

WHERE THERE IS HOPE

But is such a confident hope *biblical?* What about all the prophecies of the gloom and doom plaguing the world as history marches on? Shouldn't we just back off, defend our own little castles and timidly pray that Jesus comes back soon?

Let's look briefly at what the Word does say about the magnitude of the hope that should be central in our hearts:

Paul summarized his entire life's mission in one verse—Colossians 1:27: "To them God has chosen to make known among the Gentiles the glorious riches of this mystery, which is Christ in you, the hope of glory." Or as *The New Testament in Modern English* by J.B. Phillips puts it:

They are those to whom God has planned to give a vision of the full wonder and splendor of His secret plan for the nations. And the secret is simply this: Christ *in you!* Yes, Christ is *in you,* bringing with Him the hope of all the glorious things to come (Col. 1:27, *Phillips*).

⠼

AS THE GAP GETS DARKER, THE LIGHT SHINES BRIGHTER. THERE IS HOPE IN JESUS CHRIST, AND THROUGH HIS SALVATION, THAT HOPE IS *IN* US!

⠼

This passage assures us that:

1. Hope is *personal.* Christ Himself is the hope. No hope is available outside of Him. The hope is as big as He is.
2. Hope is *immediate.* The Christ who is our hope is "in us," or better translated "in the midst of" us. He is among His people to be all the things Colossians describes as His character and His ways.
3. Thus hope is primarily *corporate.* When Paul says Christ is in the midst of "you," the Greek word for you is plural. He is hope for all of God's people, in all ages and at all times.
4. This hope has a *missionary* dimension. It is not just for our sakes alone. It is to be proclaimed and manifested through us for the sake of the nations.
5. The hope God gives us is *profound.* It is a "mystery," Paul says. Only now is the full scope of what we have in Christ being unveiled before our eyes and before heaven and earth. But there is still much more to come. Our hope is inexhaustible.
6. Our hope in Christ deals with *ultimate issues.* It is the "hope of glory"—the hope of the full revelation of all the glorious things God has prepared for us (both now and throughout all eternity) in the person of His dear Son.
7. And that's why, for Paul, hope has become his *message* and

his ministry (see Col. 1:24,28,29). He wants to bring this hope to every person, by preaching the message of hope ("We proclaim Him," v. 28, *NASB*); by discipleship ("That we may present every man complete in Christ," v. 28, *NASB*); and by prayer ("laboring earnestly," 4:12, *NASB*). He really wants to stand in the Gap![1]

As the Gap gets darker, the light shines brighter. There is hope in Jesus Christ, and through His salvation, that hope is *in* us!

(For a full study of this passage and others related to eagerly preparing for hope, consider studying with your small group *The Hope at Hand*, using its discussion/study guide. See Resources.)

WHAT DOES A GREAT AWAKENING LOOK LIKE?

As we get ready to stand in the Gap for the cause of Christ, what exactly are we anticipating? What is revival?

For 2,000 years the knowledge of God's glory in the face of Jesus Christ (see 2 Cor. 2:14) has spread like ocean waves over the sands of peoples, languages and cultures. Some day the gospel will cover all of it. Now, in our day, God's Spirit has stirred up new surges of global outreach to thunder farther up the shore than ever before. Church historians call these waves "Great Awakenings." During the past 200 years, concurrent with the greatest missionary advance in 2 millennia, at least three such mighty rushes of God's grace have occurred. Many strategists today believe we are on the crest of another Great Awakening.

One of the foremost authorities about these waves of awakening, J. Edwin Orr, describes them in three distinct phases:

1. A spontaneous outpouring of the Holy Spirit revives Christians to the point that they band together in fervent prayer.
2. Out of united prayer meetings spring cooperative evangelism, increased lay leadership in the churches and a new zeal for present missions activity, both at home and abroad.
3. Rising from the first two phases the Church mobilizes the talents and energies of its best-trained men and women to carry

forward the missionary advance with unparalleled results.

(Dr. Orr substantiates this in three detailed volumes: *The Eager Feet, The Fervent Prayer* and *The Flaming Tongue*.)

Can it be that awakenings similar to those in the days of preacher Jonathan Edwards (early 1700s), abolitionist William Wilberforce (early 1800s) or Bishop Charles Harrison Mason (from the Church of God in Christ, early 1900s) are upon us again? Since World War II, a new crest of spiritual ferment has erupted worldwide.

As in past awakenings, people of many denominations are coming together in the Gap to seek all God wants to do through them, to throw off the shackles of unbelief and to fully commit themselves to serve the cause. In the past 35 years many in the Church have moved through phases one and two as described by Dr. Orr. What remains is the explosion of this spiritual ferment into an awakening of all God's people in the Gap, so we mobilize every resource to fill the Gap in this generation!

Missionary and seminary professor J. Christy Wilson remarked to me one morning as we met to pray: "I believe we've entered the fourth Great Awakening. It has already started—and it may be the last one. Because in this awakening God can complete His plan for the nations."

That was 20 years ago. Today, thousands of Christian leaders worldwide are saying the same thing. It can no longer be denied.

Where are we in that mounting wave of awakening? Alan Bennet, New Zealand director of OMF, says:

> To survive, the Church today has to change course. From being a chapel for the nation, it now has the potential to produce strong men and women, young and old, to stand in the Gap both at home and overseas.... In so doing, the Church becomes a skilled and readily accessed reservoir for mission anywhere on earth.
>
> True, we are plowing through a decade or two of uncertainty, where the situation remains fluid and we cannot always meet the demands of the Gap. Worse, the enemy will break through into territory once very secure. This is the time for courage, for resolute leaders and Gap-fillers at the front line.[2]

What will happen when, as Bennet puts it, "Gap-fillers" step into place to hasten a coming spiritual awakening? Theologian J.I. Packer lists several characteristics of what real revival looks like:

- An awesome sense of the presence of God;
- A profound awareness of sin, leading to both repentance and the full embrace of the glorified Christ;
- A release of the Church to witness to the power and glory of Christ, in the same freedom that the Spirit has brought to the Church through revival;
- An overflowing joy in the Lord, a love for all Christians and a fear of doing anything to violate either;
- An intensifying and speeding up of the work of grace throughout a community and throughout nations;
- Multitudes brought under conviction by the gospel and transformed by the Spirit in short order;
- Many converted and folded into the life of the Church.

Packer concludes his research into revival with the following significant observation:

> It is true, of course, that there can be personal revival without any community movement, and that there can be no community movement save as individuals are revived. Nonetheless, if we follow Acts as our paradigm, we shall define revival as an essentially corporate phenomenon in which God sovereignly shows His hand, visits His people, extends His kingdom and glorifies His name.[3]

Personal revival is great; but it only blossoms fully when dozens of believers experience personal revival, then thousands, then millions. As they come together to stand in the Gap, the hope of revival builds gradually.

In the United States alone, a mighty river of revival grows stronger and broader through the quiet input of more and more "feeder streams." What the old prophet Ezekiel wrote helps us picture this mighty river.

RIVER OF REVIVAL

Ezekiel 47:1-12

FEEDER STREAMS

- National days of prayer
- Local church initiatives
- Clergy prayer initiatives
- Citywide prayer events
- National prayer gatherings
- Multiplication of prayer ministries
- Support from books and publications
- The WORLD-WIDE prayer movement

FEEDER STREAMS

- Denominationwide initiatives
- Youth prayer initiatives
- Laypeople initiatives
- Citywide prayer movements
- National prayer-related coalitions
- Simultaneous linkage in prayer by media
- Local and national prayer initiatives for evangelism

The man brought me back to the entrance of the temple, and I saw water coming out from under the threshold of the temple toward the east (for the temple faced east). The water was coming down from under the south side of the temple, south of the altar. He then brought me out through the north gate and led me around the outside to the outer gate facing east, and the water was flowing from the south side.

As the man went eastward with a measuring line in his hand, he measured off a thousand cubits and then led me through water that was ankle-deep. He measured off another thousand cubits and led me through water that was knee-deep. He measured off another thousand and led me through water that was up to the waist. He measured off another thousand, but now it was a river that I could not cross, because the water had risen and was deep enough to swim in—a river that no one could cross. He asked me, "Son of man, do you see this?" Then he led me back to the bank of the river. When I arrived there, I saw a great number of trees on each side of the river. He said to me, "This water flows toward the eastern region and goes down into the Arabah, where it enters the Sea. When it empties into the Sea, the water there becomes fresh. Swarms of living creatures will live wherever the river flows. There will be large numbers of fish, because this water flows there and makes the salt water fresh; so where the river flows everything will live. Fishermen will stand along the shore; from En Gedi to En Eglaim there will be places for spreading nets. The fish will be of many kinds—like the fish of the Great Sea. But the swamps and marshes will not become fresh; they will be left for salt. Fruit trees of all kinds will grow on both banks of the river. Their leaves will not wither, nor will their fruit fail. Every month they will bear, because the water from the sanctuary flows to them. Their fruit will serve for food and their leaves for healing.

The full river of revival may not have arrived yet, but the feeder streams are very active. So I ask you: Can the river be very far ahead? The hope of revival makes it well worth the risk of standing in the Gap. Our stand for Jesus Christ spurs others on to hope, to an eager anticipation of revival sweeping the United States. We become messengers of hope.

EXAMPLES FROM THE PAST

Messengers of the hope of revival have been around since the apostles preached on Pentecost to the nations gathered in Jerusalem; since Philip, a Jew, planted churches in Samaritan villages and then shared the gospel with an international visitor from Ethiopia; since Peter crossed the threshold between Jews and Gentiles to bring Christ to a Roman centurion and his family.

The New Testament is full of messengers of hope:

- The members of the Jerusalem Church scattered abroad by persecution, preaching the message to Jews and Greeks as well;
- Paul and Barnabas sent out by the Church at Antioch to establish other churches throughout Galatia;
- Aquila and Priscilla who formed the nucleus of a mission-minded church that evangelized all of Asia Minor in less than three years;
- The Thessalonian Church whose life together established a witness that reached far beyond them into Macedonia and Achaia;
- John banished to an island dungeon because he proclaimed Christ in the face of great political and theological barriers, but given there a prophet's overview of the global climax of the Christian movement.

These believers turned the world upside down (see Acts 17:6)!

Thousands of other messengers of hope have preceded us in the Gap. A fourth-century Christian, John Chrysostom, stood in the Gap for the barbarian Goths of the Balkans, training and sending missionaries to reach them. He defined God's vision for his life this way:

> We have a whole Christ for our salvation, a whole Bible for our staff, a whole Church for our fellowship and a whole world for our parish.

Patrick stood in the Gap for the Celtic people in Ireland to plant the Church there in the fifth century. In the sixth century, Columbia, building on this foundation, founded a missions community off the Irish coast on the island of Iona where Celtic believers were trained and sent into the Gap between the gospel and the unreached tribes of Northern Europe.

In the thirteenth century a youthful messenger of hope named Francis left his family's wealth in Assisi, Italy, to stand in the Gap. Initially he and his wandering band worked in a narrower part of the Gap in Europe, but gradually the Franciscan Order became a movement that renewed the Church and reached around the globe!

Another messenger-of-hope movement, the Dominicans, produced compassionate Bartolome de las Casas. In the 1500s he stood in the Gap for Indians oppressed by the Spanish in the New World. He worked for their conversion and struggled with the Spanish government to institute laws that secured their humane treatment. Later, a Puritan, John Eliot, gave his life in the Gap on behalf of abused Native Americans and slaves in America.

The Moravians were a society made up of families from Bohemia who sought political refuge in Germany. During the eighteenth century, they sent out "revival teams" to cities throughout Europe and England calling Christians to get ready for the outpouring of the Holy Spirit. They also sent out other teams of messengers of hope to stand in the Gap for peoples in North America, South America, Africa and China, as well as other parts of Europe.

Those Moravians who did the "sending" were standing in the Gap just as fully as those who went. For example, their German sending base sponsored a 24-hour prayer chain that lasted almost 100 years! The chain backed their commitment to send forth 10 percent of their number.

The Gap-filler we call "the father of modern missions" was an ordinary cobbler who met monthly in the late 1700s with a small group to pray for "the revival of religion and the expansion of Christ's kingdom around the world." William Carey caught a big-picture vision. His own research on the Gap, entitled *An Enquiry into the Obligations of Christians to Use Means for the Conversion of the Heathen* is an explosive volume that describes his findings about millions of unreached peoples who lay captive and oppressed at the Gap's widest end.

William Carey's little book turned English Christians around and broke the logjam in protestant missionary efforts that had blighted the cause since the Reformation. Eventually, Carey relocated to another part of the Gap to obey his world vision on behalf of India. He translated Scriptures into more than 30 languages and planted churches throughout Calcutta.

But those who hastened the tide of revival in their day were not all great names in Church history; they were not all "revivalists" or pioneering missionaries. Some were simple unknowns who have changed the course of history by standing in the Gap—ordinary believers like us—standing in the ways we will explore in this book.

The following is how a friend of mine named Bruce describes his own "conversion" while at M.I.T. to the kind of activist Christianity that stands in the Gap:

> After I had realized that Jesus Christ was Lord, I became aware that He wanted to use my life to reach others. I was, in fact, useful to Him. This had tremendous ramifications in the choices of future occupations in my life. Even beyond this, there came a point in my growth as a Christian when I realized that Jesus wasn't just for me. Jesus Christ was desiring that I help make Him known to the ends of the earth.... No longer could I keep Him for myself or be content with making Him known to a few friends and those like me, but He was desiring to use me to help make Him known to people different from myself. The scope of His concerns and now, therefore, my concerns was the world.

HOW IT HAPPENED TO ME

You're probably wondering by now how I personally became such a fanatic about getting ready for a coming national and world revival—how it was that I started standing in the Gap.

Some time ago I was leading a three-day conference about standing in the Gap. During Sunday lunch a businessman shared with me how he had been depressed the entire weekend. Finally he had figured out why.

As he caught a vision that weekend, he realized he had spent the past two years as a new Christian without Christ's cause as his highest priority. He had been living the Christian life for what he could get out of it, and he deeply regretted the lost time. But I told him that nothing was lost. All of his growth as Jesus' disciple would be valuable as he now took his stand with Him in the Gap.

"Be grateful it was only 2 years," I said. "Many have labored 10 to 20 years at Christian discipleship without making this great discovery."

I was one of those. When I became a Christian my freshman year in college, I thrived on Bible study, sang my heart out with newly found hymns, drank in the fresh warmth of Christian fellowship for the first time, but ran scared from the missions study group on campus. That's where my pilgrimage toward being a messenger of hope began.

And I kept on running! Right through undergraduate studies in religion and graduate studies in theology, I successfully avoided every missions course that was offered along the way. There was something about the whole topic that seemed dull, peculiar, and above all, threatening to my own plans for Christian service. I was stuck in pea-sized Christianity, boxed off from the thrill of Christ's global cause by my Gap of Unbelief.

But the Lord Jesus wanted for me exactly what He wanted for His first disciples: that I catch a world vision and move out on it. My discovery of this began when, during my years of graduate study, He put me into an inner-city Bible club ministry in the neighborhoods of South Chicago. At first I was unaware of what was happening to me. But there Christ gave me a vision for people where the Gap was much wider than I had experienced before. He also showed me materially poor Christians who were passionately fulfilling the call of Ezekiel 22:30 in their own backyards.

In the late '60s, He led me into the pastorate in Kent, Ohio, and cracked open my pea-sized boxes even more. For six years He helped me discover the potential of a local congregation to make a citywide as well as a worldwide impact for His cause.

Just as many other pastors, I struggled to give meaningful leadership to our church's involvement with three or four missionaries. I had never met any of them. It was difficult to teach my church how to pray for them. I knew little about the big picture of what God was doing beyond my church myself and had little desire to find out, with few clues about where to begin. But God had a surprise for me!

Because our church was located by Ohio's Kent State University, many students from Christian campus organizations attended our services. To connect these students with our church families, we began what we called our "adoption program."

As the years passed God sent many of our "adopted" students into other parts of the United States and into other countries in the world. We woke up to this fact the year we placed a map on the wall of our educational wing marked with flags representing the places our student friends came from and the places they were going.

Multiplying those flags during the previous five years of ministry and seeing how we were literally touching the ends of the earth was simply overwhelming. (Incidentally, I would recommend that any student fellowship or local church take a map and try the same experiment. A new perspective on how to fit into God's plan for the nations will be gained.)

Without our realizing it, God had placed our church right in the middle of a ministry to train agents of revival! The possibilities were unlimited. And, the vital link between the church as a base and the students was the families who adopted them. As students and young couples from our midst went forth in many capacities, our whole church could make a lasting contribution to the cause of revival. The training we gave them, the quality of community life we showed them and the deep support they received from individual family units would go with them. We could become a church of senders and goers—all standing in the Gap.

Then from Kent, Ohio, shots were heard around the world. May 1970 found the United States in the midst of tumultuous demonstrations against American involvement in the Vietnam conflict. As I stood on the Commons at Kent State, National Guard bullets struck down four students.

In the stunned aftermath, I watched as individuals involved in something in one small part of the world rocked a whole generation and affected the consciousness of nations toward a war. For some time after the shootings, people traveled from everywhere to declare their solidarity with those who died, with a life-and-death cause of international proportions.

The parallels of this tragedy to the mission of Christ were obvious. I thought: *Could not a local group of students and church laypeople bound together for the sake of the Gap have a similarly far-reaching impact on Christ's global cause?*

All this created in me a longing to expand my own world vision to lead our church. My hunger grew as I met with concerned laymen to pray eight hours each week for six weeks about our church's future. We studied through the book of Ephesians—a theology of the revival. We used one chapter each week as the basis for which we praised and petitioned God. One evidence of what God taught us throughout those days was the motto He gave for our church: "Applying the gospel of Christ to the world of Kent—and the world beyond."

My hunger to know more about standing in the Gap for Christ's global cause increased in 1970 when my wife Robyne and I attended InterVarsity's Urbana Student Missions Convention in Illinois. At that convention, we met with many mission agencies and heard great sermons about the overall mission of the Church. There was hope for the world!

In 1973 my hunger took a more personal turn through a mentoring relationship God gave me with a Buddhist Japanese student doing graduate work in the Kent State physics department. I saw the hope of the gospel plant deep roots in him.

Through all these experiences I was becoming what we called a "world Christian"—a believer with a vision beyond myself, a vision for Christ's global cause. Finally it happened. Becoming a World Christian took me out of the pastorate! The situation had created in me such a craving to know more about Christ's worldwide mission that I knew I wouldn't be satisfied until I understood.

Leaving behind financial security, a fulfilling ministry and the comfort of family and friends, Robyne and I ventured to Southern California to spend a year at Fuller Seminary's School of World Mission. Not only did God provide for every physical need (That's a story in itself!), but He also built in us the world vision we longed for. For nine months of classes I sat at the feet of leading mission strategists; furloughed missionaries (with a combined 1,500 years of missionary experience); and church leaders from the Two-Thirds World, committed to biblical revival.

Like the businessman I mentioned before, I too experienced a time of depression during those months as I realized how much my previous 12 years as a Christian had lacked. I was hit hard by statistical studies and multimedia presentations describing the 1 billion people who were starving physically and the 2 billion who had never heard the name of Christ. Even in our own country of America, millions who had never heard were arriving as international workers, students, refugees and immigrants. They only added to the more than 100 million Americans who themselves were "without hope and without God" (Eph. 2:12). And I saw that only a revived Church could ever fill this Gap.

Why should this be? And, why wasn't I given the big picture before? Then the harder questions began to bombard my mind: *Was I willing to open up to these people? Was I willing to love them? Was I willing to seek God for a greater work of His Spirit in my generation? What changes would this make in my life?*

As a Christian, I'd mostly structured my life around other Christians. I had the us-and-them mentality. I had very few real relationships with the "them," especially those nonbelievers not like me.

What would it mean for me to stand in the Gap? What would it mean for me to live seeking revival? And for Robyne and our marriage? What impact could the two of us have on a pre-revived church, and for unreached peoples with such compelling needs? How would we get started?

Fortunately, during this time God put us with other Christians who had caught the same vision and were working through the same questions. We labored together to build our vision, to learn how to put it into practice in very practical ways and how to pass it along to others. Many kinds of world-sized ministries sprang from that fellowship of "world Christians."

Since then the global cause of the living Christ has continued to transform my life. Not only in terms of occupation and ministry, but even in marriage. Robyne and I have seen the effects of this grand discovery. The broad sweep of being messengers of hope to a world of hopelessness has become the context for our relationship—and it has transformed everything for us.

For example, our prayer life continues to grow in its focus on others rather than mostly ourselves. We pray for national revival, global revival, for missionaries, unreached people groups and about current international events. Our new priorities have changed everything from what magazines we take to the kinds of social events we attend. And we've poured our lives out for nearly 20 years to mobilize "world Christians" into united prayer for personal and wide-scale awakening to Christ—in hundreds of cities around the globe.

We also want to save our time and money for those things that will help us to obey our world vision. We delayed investing in a house, for example, until we thought God had moved us where He wanted us to settle for a time of maximum involvement in the Gap. Then we purchased in a neighborhood where the Gap is culturally wider than in other parts of town.

Deciding to stand in the Gap has influenced our hospitality ministry. Often we invite other messengers of hope expressly to build our vision together, or potential Gap-fillers to help them catch the vision. Our guests include believers from church backgrounds completely different from our own. We host urban ministry workers and missionaries from the front lines to refresh them and learn from them. We invite non-Christian internationals who just "happen" to live nearby so we can love a few at the Gap's widest end.

Eventually three other "guests" joined us permanently: an abandoned child from Kerala, South India, named Adam; beautiful Bethany from an orphanage near Puna in the north; and our youngest, Benjamin, also from Puna. Robyne and I adopted each because God set them before us and called us to love them as our own. (We were delighted to comply!)

Of course, some people don't understand all this, or us. But stretching back 2,000 years stands a great company of disciples who do—agents of revival, world Christians, messengers of hope—standing in the Gap. Do you see them? We do. And that's enough for us, for now.

Notes

1. David Bryant, *The Hope at Hand* (Grand Rapids: Baker Books, 1995), pp. 39-41. Segment used by permission.

2. Alan Bennett, "The Gap Revisited," *East Asia's Millions* (December 1996-January/February 1997): 14,16.

3. J.I. Packer, *A Quest for Godliness: The Puritan Vision of the Christian Life* (Wheaton, Ill.: Crossway Books, 1990), p. 36.

3 | RETREATING FROM THE GAP: THE CURSE OF PEA-SIZED CHRISTIANITY

BOXES THAT BLIND US
TO THE HOPE BEFORE US

▓

Comedian Woody Allen quipped, "Mankind is caught at a crossroads. One road leads to hopelessness and despair, and the other leads to total annihilation. Let us pray we have the wisdom to choose rightly!"

That kind of pessimism pervades much of the American Church today. Believers are hunching down behind barriers as our culture seems to get more and more evil. They feel they cannot control anything out there, but at least they can protect themselves and their families.

But is defensiveness a mark of biblical discipleship? Believers who are fearful about the future and what a disintegration of our culture might do to them are forgetting that God has not given us a spirit of fear, "but a spirit of power, of love and of self-discipline" (2 Tim. 1:7).

Fortunately, what happens with America does not ultimately determine what happens with God's plan for the nations; Christ's Church is worldwide. But unfortunately, many Christians in the West are not keeping pace with the Kingdom's worldwide expansion. Many of us are sleeping right through the hope at hand—the promise of coming revival. We are like those who lived at the time of Christ on earth and still did not "recognize the time of God's coming" (Luke 19:44)!

THE GREATEST OF ALL GAPS

The tendency for Christians to be fearful is not a new issue, however. It has been with us a long time. And this tendency delays the joy of revival and the discipling of the nations—our own included.

Why, with more than a third of a million churches in America, hasn't true, good-news Christianity penetrated the fields of science, politics and the media—much less penetrated the homes within our neighborhoods? Why in a country whose motto is "In God We Trust" are citizens prone to racial hatred, dependency upon drugs, addiction, pornography and despair? Why, after 2,000 years of countless possibilities for world evangelization by an international Church, are more than 2 billion people still unevangelized, most of whom have not even heard Christ's name?

One answer is unavoidable. The single greatest Gap among the nations is between God's promise to bless the nations through Christ's disciples (see Gen. 12:3, 18:18, etc.) and the faith of those disciples to claim that promise and act on it. It's the *Gap of Unbelief.*

This Gap of Unbelief puts limits on what Christ will do through us. We wonder: *Can He really use me as an agent of revival within a nation facing impending judgment?* On top of that, *can He really reach the ends of the earth through people like us at a time like this?*

We're often like the citizens of the town of Nazareth, "[Jesus] did not do many miracles there because of their unbelief" (Matt. 13:58, *NASB*). God's indictment for the lack of faith in Ezekiel's generation positions itself at the front steps of my church, too: "but I found none" (22:30).

Further, our Gap of Unbelief makes us hesitate to take bold risks for the cause of Christ. We wonder: *If we lose our lives for Christ, will we ever see any lasting returns worth our investment?*

Our Gap of Unbelief turns us from the many possibilities to fulfill our destinies as salt and light and focuses our attention instead on our own self-preservation. We wonder: *How can we worry about billions of unreached people when we have so many personal needs that might go unmet in the process?*

Our Gap of Unbelief blinds us to the dreams, resources and strategies God would give us to bridge the Gap in our ministry of "reconciling men to God" (see 2 Cor. 5:18-20)—in our cities, across our nation, before our generation.

If once aroused by the presence and power of Christ's mighty Spirit, what could hold us back?

Yet in the Gap of Unbelief, down through history and in the Church today, the constant battle has been to get Christians to push forward, stop whining, stop resting, wake up, stand together and take hold of the victorious hope Christ has given us for our own people and for the world.

Why has unbelief persisted to stifle the momentum of the Christian movement again and again? Camouflaged within the Gap of Unbelief hides a culprit I call "pea-sized Christianity."

BOXES OF PEA-SIZED CHRISTIANITY

When Peter opposed Christ's expressed mission to the cross (see Matt. 16:21-23), he was told, in effect, "Get out of my way, Satan. You are a hindrance to me. You're approaching this mission from a human perspective, not God's." Peter was still in his own box of pea-sized Christianity.

Pea-sized Christianity comes in boxes of many shapes and sizes, and at least one box can fit any Christian who allows it. These boxes keep us from the hope of revival, from a discipleship that is big enough to flood a world-sized Gap. You don't find very many rivers in a box!

For example, there are pea-sized boxes called:

- *Convert Christianity.* Life in Christ gets no bigger than making it safely inside the Kingdom.
- *Character Christianity.* Life in Christ gets no bigger than pulling one's own spiritual act together.
- *Consumption Christianity.* Life in Christ is boxed up into meeting one's own personal needs—and that's all.
- *Cloister Christianity.* Life in Christ is no bigger than the warm secure fellowship I have each week with my good Christian buddies.
- *Career Christianity.* Life in Christ is no bigger for me than getting nicely settled into a well-paying job—and then realizing the career is a subtle sort of trap.
- *Church Christianity.* Life in Christ has grown no bigger than the Sunday School picnic, the choir's Christmas

pageant, the monthly finance committee meetings or scouting out who is absent from midweek prayer service.

- *Culture Christianity* is a form of pea-sized Christianity that affects all of us to some degree. In this box our life in Christ grows no bigger than a North American, ethnic-specific, class-specific brand of worship, and a witness that says, "Be a nice person, stick with nice people—the ones who look just like me." We relish in our tried-and-true traditions, which we erroneously equate with the eternal ways of the Kingdom itself.

In summary, when my Christian experience expands no further than my salvation, my small group, my church or my future, it is pea sized. When I compartmentalize my walk with Christ into neat packages of do's and don'ts, it is pea sized. When I remain unreconciled with my Hispanic, African-American or Asian brothers and sisters in Christ, my

::

MANY CHRISTIANS HAVE GROWN INTO SPIRITUAL AGORAPHOBICS—DISCIPLES WHO WOULD RATHER STAY IN THE SECURITY OF A BOX THAN VENTURE OUT WITH CHRIST INTO HIS RADICAL, ADVENTUROUS CAUSE.

::

love for Christ Himself is still pea sized. When my activities and interests don't vitally link me to being an agent of revival, for standing in the Gap on behalf of others, I have succumbed to pea-sized Christianity.

Of course, concentrating on outreach to the neglect of our personal needs and the needs of the Christians around us can also be a pea-sized affair. I am not arguing that we leap from one box into another. Rather, I am suggesting that we need a *new context* for praying, worshiping, Bible study, employing spiritual gifts, racial reconciliation and even for evangelism. That context is the Gap. We need its big-picture dimension for our discipleship.

As many as 2.5 million Americans today suffer from the most common and disabling of all phobias—agoraphobia, the fear of open spaces and unfamiliar situations. Often they have grown up believing the outside world is so dangerous and unmanageable that it is better to stick to familiar routines and only rarely to venture alone outside the house.

Similarly, many Christians have grown into spiritual agoraphobics—disciples who would rather stay in the security of a box than venture out with Christ into His radical, adventurous cause. How can anything they do advance God's kingdom as long as this disorder goes unchecked?

Tragically, little place exists in our thinking for national and world revival when our daily discipleship runs on pea-sized dreams and strategies! Just as tragic: We don't discover the thrill of God using us to close the great Gap between Himself and billions who by sin are separated from His love. We rarely even think about it. In the end, we contribute little to God's highest priority for this hour of history.

Fortunately, Christ did not save us to store us in boxes of pea-sized Christianity! He has laid hold of us to stand with Him in the Gap! So why do we settle for less? Why are we afraid to follow Him when He is building His Church, and the gates of Hades will not overcome it (see Matt. 16:18)? Maybe because of *narcissism, smörgasborditis* and plain old *blindness*.

REASONS FOR THE BOXES

1. Narcissism. Face it: We easily succumb to the current mood of our society, and the mood of our society is generally cynical.

Gallup polls recently illustrated Americans' pessimism in the nation. About 78 percent of Americans agree that "our leaders are more concerned with managing their images than with solving our nation's problems." The researchers reported their findings to the National Commission on Civic Renewal, a group addressing "perceived moral decline in society and growing disaffection."

In response to the report, former Education Secretary William J. Bennett asked the researchers, "Did you ask them, then, why they watch TV 25 hours a week, get divorced and don't take responsibility for their children?"

"They do not implicate themselves," replied the survey team.[1]

In the uncertainty of global economics and post-Cold War politics, we Americans tend to blame uncontrollable outside forces for our problems and then turn inward, where we can at least try to control our own lives. We can become so self-focused that, as the mythical Narcissus gazing at his own reflection, we become paralyzed.

Even many Christians in the United States have given up on personally attempting anything significant in the Gap. Narcissism has spawned fear and unbelief in the Church.

As a result, we tend to opt for an undisturbed retreat into our boxes. We rationalize, "There's no use trying to face the complex challenges of the world today. It's all so far beyond ordinary people like us. Let's concentrate instead on loving each other, or those nearest us who are easiest to love. Maybe that's all we have a right to do."

Think for a moment: How much goes on in local churches that is just basic self-preservation and a fearful retreat, reflective of the rest of our society?

2. Smörgasborditis. Another reason we've settled for pea-sized Christianity is the evangelical affluence of the United States. Christians smother our faith. Frankly, most of us suffer from overindulgence in the variety of spiritual food around us.

Scores of organized discipleship programs are available in and out of the local church on which to feast, along with a wealth of Christian books, magazines, radio programs and cassettes dealing with every conceivable issue or personal problem. Famous personalities entertain us at deeper-life concerts and seminars. We can sample an abundance of options for local Christian ministries with all the trimmings needed to pull them off with ease. And for dessert a whole menu of charities and organizations are ready to help us painlessly discharge any guilt about the pleas of the needy; we can simply pull out the checkbook and discharge our accountability in the Gap!

We become spiritually obese when we saturate ourselves with such a scrumptious input but are devoid of sufficient exercise in output. Some have described this as "nominal evangelicalism." We act and look as if we are committed to standing in the Gap, but we are actually "nominal" when it comes to doing a lot about it.

Often we are encouraged to pick and choose from the delightful array of Christian growth opportunities as if we are at an all-you-can-eat buffet, a smörgasbord. We nibble on those things that fit our schedules, our needs and our interests. In the process, we pass right over God's timetable for revival. Smörgasborditis makes us oblivious to needs that are much greater than our own. With so many blessings to choose from at home, we are not motivated to choose a sacrificial involvement in others' destinies. In fact, most of us are afraid of all we suspect it will cost us.

3. Blindness. As American believers, we certainly are not stupid. We are often just ignorant—"not knowing." A third reason we have stayed in boxes of pea-sized Christianity is our basic ignorance of the facts. This blindness may be our fundamental problem.

What is our problem? In a nutshell: We see the world differently from the way God does. We haven't quite caught His plan, His vision and His hope for our nation and this world. Until we do, we will never fully understand what our roles can be in the challenge He has set before us.

We don't know where we've been. Honestly now, how many of us even *know* we are living in the Gap? How often is our vision and courage to stand in the Gap stirred by a gripping lesson on those that have stood before us? If we don't know where we've been, do we know where we are now in God's historic plan? How ignorant are we of the lessons learned throughout Church history? Do we know anything of the sweeping revivals that have transformed the global advance of the gospel into the longest sustained spiritual enterprise in human history?

Writing in *The Essential Components for World Evangelization,* Ralph Winter said:

> We need a special education just to know the uncensored facts of our world today. The [expansion of the Church] is not a simple phenomenon. Common impressions are mainly wrong.... A Christian student may be able to get a course on the history of jazz, but very few state universities or even Christian liberal arts colleges offer a course precisely on the history of the Christian mission.... I am almost more concerned about what the schools do *not* teach rather than what they *do* teach. Attacks and criticisms we can grapple with, but the total absence of data is much more subtle and difficult to handle.... There is no way that evangelicalism in

America has any serious future if 90 percent of its younger generation is being undermined on a wholesale basis year after year into the future.[2]

Not only are many of us ignorant of our past as the family of God; we further have a skewed idea of what is happening right now in our world. As I travel to churches and campuses nationwide, I find few believers actually studying the daily newspaper, let alone catching up on the news about God's expanding Kingdom throughout the world today. A college student's coursework may teach him or her about global economics, international relations, unusual cultures and the arts in 30 countries; but students even in Christian schools often learn little about what God is doing in world revival.

Of course, Satan's job is to "deceive the whole world" (Rev. 12:9, *NASB*), and he is an expert at using the high-tech American communications systems for doing just that. He temporarily deceives even the elect by ensuring that we never hear the message of hope, the good news about what God is doing in our country and our world.

For example, has the six o'clock news or your daily newspaper ever hinted at what God is doing—such as:

In the mid-'90s, over a 3-day period Billy Graham proclaimed the gospel to more than 1 billion people and trained 1 million Christian workers via satellite. In Cairo, Egypt alone, all 346 evangelical churches participated in the satellite broadcasts. With 106,000 Egyptian viewers, about 9,000 on each of the 3 days responded to the claims of Christ!

Today, missionaries are from everywhere to everywhere. Indian churches are sending more than 11,000 cross-cultural workers. Korean missionaries increased from 160 in 1984 to over 5,000 today. Kenya is supporting 2,166 missionaries and Nigeria 2,878 of its own missionaries!

The harvest is vast! One mission agency alone—Every Home for Christ—recently reported an increase from 426,000 decisions for Christ in one year to 1,500,000 just two years later!

The Body of Christ in the United States is now sending out about 200,000 short-term missionaries every year!

Remember the good old days when giving to missions was a priority? Well, these are the good old days, since American believers are giving 5 percent more to foreign mission than 25 years ago.

In a recent "Say Yes, Chicago" evangelistic emphasis, some 135,000 Chicagoans attended 70 coordinated events —with more than 9,000 coming to faith in Christ!

The number of Latin American Protestant believers mushroomed from about 18 million to nearly 60 million during the past 10 years—a 220 percent increase.

Canadian Chinese are helping to plant new Chinese churches—in Venezuela! Elsewhere along the northern coast in Guyana, one of the most effective evangelism tools among the Chinese is a Dutch comic book series about the Bible. These Dutch-speaking Chinese in South America who came to Christ through comics have formed a church and sent their first mission team to plant a new church—in French Guyana!

One and one-half million believers marched together through the streets of Sao Paulo, Brazil, to proclaim Jesus as Lord over their city!

Every three years The European Mission Association (TEMA) hosts about 7,000 youth at its student mission conference. Just one effort in Germany is now sending out 50 short-term mission teams in a new German mission movement.

During a recent five-year period, more than 1,500 churches of new believers were started across England. Throughout the 1980s an average of one church per week had closed in this country. In the '90s, however, two new churches started each week! In the mid-'90s, virtually every denomination within the Body of Christ in England committed together to plant 20,000 new churches and see 20 percent of the population attending church by the year 2000.

In France, about 70,000 Gypsies have become evangelical, born-again believers in Christ. Pray for their powerful witness to the other quarter-million Gypsies in France.

About 15,000 Muslims each year now convert to Christianity in Egypt, where new believers are heavily persecuted.

In a one-year period the *JESUS* film was shown to more than 1.6 million people throughout the Islamic country of Sudan in North Africa. In the southern region where Christians have been beaten and some even crucified for their faith, 180,000 viewed the film and 120,000 indicated that they wanted to follow Jesus.

In Zambia an average 1,000 people per day die of AIDS in this small country. In Zambia as well as in northeastern Zimbabwe, teams of Baptist believers go and preach at the AIDS funerals—three-day ceremonies involving thousands. More than two dozen new churches have so far been planted in this way.

In Malawi, a country with the highest AIDS rate in the world (It was reported in 1996 that one-third of the population would be dead from AIDS by A.D. 2000.), a radical spiritual awakening among Anglicans erupted when a diocese bishop publicly repented for his sins and made a first-time commitment to Christ. The Episcopal Church Mission Committee reports: "Since then, 200,000 Anglicans have made personal commitments to Jesus!"

Throughout a recent four-year period in Russia, 36 million Scriptures were distributed in classrooms. More than 110,000 students and their parents have seen the *JESUS* film. And 125,000 teachers and school administrators have attended training seminars about biblical ethics and morality. *Moscovskij Komsomolets,* the official Russian Communist Party youth newspaper since 1919, published a report about Easter celebrations in a recent April issue. Editors placed above the newspaper's banner in large letters: "CHRIST IS RISEN"!

During the mid-'90s about 2,500 Christian workers from throughout the Himalayas met in Nepal to make cooperative plans to evangelize Nepal, Sikkim, Bhutan and northern India. Nepali believers, only a few in the 1950s, now number from 200,000 to 300,000. The deputy chief minister, superintendent of police and chief administrator of Sikkim attended the conference and estimated that at that time fully 20 percent of the population of Sikkim had become believers in Christ!

Throughout a recent 12-month period in India, 20,000 new believers were baptized among the Malto and Santal peoples in Bihar—an area renowned for 200 years as "the graveyard of missions"!

Recently in India, Promise Keepers' point man Bill McCartney and Pastor Wellington Boone challenged 4,000 pastors to repent for the sin of the caste mentality. The response was two hours of weeping and crying. The rally was part of a realistic (for Asians!) plan to train 100,000 workers to plant 1.4 million new churches within five years.

The leading Islamic periodical *Al-Muslimoon* published the article "Faith Tragedy in Bangladesh" with the subhead, "Thousands of Muslims Converted to Christianity—3,000 in the Region of Chittagong." Studied as a religious social phenomenon by Sheikh Mohammed Akhtar Husain, dean of the Arabic Language College at Kashif University, the conversion, the article states, "is not external appearances only as have been noted in some previous group conversions. The new Christians threw their copies of the Qur'an and lifted the Injils [New Testaments] high over their heads."

In Myanmar (Burma), pastors trained in intensive 4-day church-planting schools are starting churches throughout the country. To qualify for the follow-up Bible training, student pastors must see at least five come to faith in Christ. One graduate wrote to the Singapore training agency, "I do not have five converts. But I have 70...." Pray for these hundreds of thousands of unsung heroes of the faith scattered throughout the Two-Thirds World!

"Christianity fever has been sweeping all of China

throughout the past few years," reports the Chinese Church Research Center in Hong Kong. One group of elderly "Bible women" provides some of that awareness as they travel from province to province declaring "Gospel Months." They report, "The way we operate during Gospel Month is we demand that every believer lead at least one person to the Lord. For example, if there are 100,000 believers in one area, they will lead another 100,000 people to Christ during that time. There the number of believers will multiply 100 percent."

Following the Korean Conflict, South Korea was so poor that a pastor couldn't afford paper and had to write his sermon notes on discarded wrapping paper. Today, South Korea is one of the four East Asian "Dragons" enjoying unprecedented economic growth. Why? The 35 percent of its population who are Christians know the answer is prayer. Dawn prayer meetings, all-night prayer watches, loud congregational prayers—a Filipino observer says Koreans' "individual prayer lives have been a rebuke to multitudes of [our Filipino] churches." About 500 facilities are specifically dedicated to prayer and fasting—prayer retreat sites, prayer mountains, prayer gardens and prayer houses. One prayer mountain in Osanri has more than 20,000 Koreans per day coming to pray!

Oh, and that poor pastor who couldn't afford paper 40 years ago? That was Paul Yonggi Cho, former pastor of the world's largest church with 830,000 members! With 10 of the world's 20 largest churches in the capital city of Seoul—which is 40 percent believers—with 65 percent of the Army Christian, with the largest theological seminaries in the world, with the largest face-to-face meeting in history (2.7 million attended a prayer mobilization rally), with 85,000 to 105,000 students recently committing themselves to mission work—can the rest of us in the Body learn a lesson? Prayer is the key!

Since 1974, the Philippines' 5,000 evangelical churches have multiplied into 29,000. One such church is the 15-

year-old Jesus Is Lord Fellowship with 200,000 members.
The Philippine Council of Evangelical Churches reports
that 20 percent of the Philippines' population is now
evangelical Christian. The city of Manila was publicly dedicated to Christ, with the mayor symbolically giving Jesus
the key to the city. More than 1 million believers attended
the dedication![3]

Okay. Let me pause so you can catch your breath! Inhaling any hope
yet?

Can you see why lacking facts about the big picture of what God is
doing in His Word, in His work and in His world allows Christians to
form all kinds of justifications for not standing in the Gap? The *myths*
behind these justifications include:

- The Gap is pretty well closed already—as if all our churches are revived, as if everyone in America has been presented the gospel and ministered to in the name of Jesus, as if
  the world with its 10,000 remaining unreached people
  groups has already been reached.
- If we are realistic, the Gap is too wide to ever be closed.
  Unless we are hopeless idealists, we should simply give up.
- The Second Coming is really God's way to close the global
  Gap, so we can relax. Of course, this is a concept based
  only on a partial report of the biblical facts.
- Too much attention on the Gap will disrupt my own solid
  spiritual growth. Any knowledge of the expansion of the
  Church through history would quell this myth!
- When God is ready to close the Gap, He will do it without
  much help from any of us. But unless I'm mistaken, the
  Bible quotes something about "So send I you."
- Some Christians stand in the Gap, while the rest of us
  "work for a living." Only super-spiritual people would even
  dare to stand there, and these "professional Christians" are
  few and far between.

In response to these myths, let me give you a folksy proverb: "God cannot lead us out of boxes of pea-sized Christianity on the basis of facts we do not know and refuse to learn."

GET OUT

Narcissism, smörgasborditis, blindness—all these have kept the Gap of Unbelief alive for too many of us too long. As a result, we have remained in our boxes of pea-sized Christianity. But God doesn't intend that we persist in this useless condition!

The "Lausanne Covenant," embraced by zealous believers from nearly 200 nations at several International Congresses of World Evangelization within the past three decades, affirms God's desire for all of us to break out of the boxes of pea-sized Christianity with the following affirmation:

> We affirm that Christ sends His redeemed people into the world as the Father sent Him, and that this calls for a similar deep and costly penetration of the world. We must break out of our ecclesiastical ghettos and permeate our society.

He who gave His own Son to close the Sin Gap between ourselves and God, also yearns for a people who will effectively keep pace with the critical hour in which He has placed us. In the American part of the global Body of Christ, He is looking for believers with the courage to embrace the hope of coming revival, of a spiritual awakening in our churches and hometowns. That coming revival will raise up millions more who will stand by faith with Christ in His fight—until the Gap of opportunity is closed throughout the earth.

If you are in a box of pea-sized Christianity, *get out!*

Notes
1. Associated Press, "Reality Versus Values—A Middle-Class Dilemma" Colorado Springs *Gazette Telegraph* (January 20, 1997) p. A15.
2. Ralph Winter, *The Essential Components for World Evangelization* (Pasadena, Calif.: William Carey Library, 1980), pp. 12-14.
3. Bill and Amy Stearns, *Global Reports*, World Christian Inc., various issues 1996.

4 | Thriving in the Gap: What It Means to Be a "Prisoner of Hope"

Getting Serious About Revival

▪

What shall we call this perspective that can change us so radically that we move out beyond our old pea-sized boxes to stand in the Gap? Agents of revival? World Christians?

The Old Testament prophet Zechariah wrote of God's promise to us as "prisoners of hope":

> As for you, because of the blood of my covenant with you, I will free your prisoners from the waterless pit. Return to your fortress, O prisoners of hope; even now I announce that I will restore twice as much to you (Zech. 9:11,12).

Because of Christ's cross, God is forever in the business of transforming "prisoners of waterless pits" into "prisoners of hope." Not just any kind of hope, either. In this context, Zechariah is talking about nothing less than the supreme hope of both personal and widespread revival.

One observer of the Second Great Awakening (in the late 1700s and early 1800s) described the revival that resulted in the modern missionary movement. Ebenezer Porter recorded this eyewitness conclusion in his 1830 book, *Lectures on Revival:*

The history of these revivals shows that the genuine tendency of such seasons is to render Christians grateful, watchful and fervent in spirit.... When the Redeemer comes in the triumphs of His grace to visit His churches, then His true followers are seen waking from their apathy, and going forth to welcome the King of Zion with an energy and earnestness and ardor of affection greatly surpassing their first love.

What God has done before, He is very willing and ready to do again—and even *more*.

REVIVAL—NOT JUST SURVIVAL

Many of us have been living our days satisfied if we can simply "hold down the fort" until Jesus returns. We are exhausted, confused, disappointed and fearful—bent on survival, not revival.

But the Spirit of God has a better idea: the gift of hope. Any Christian who is living in the fullness of God's power abounds in hope (see Rom. 15:13); he or she sets his or her heart on hope (see 1 Pet. 1:13); he or she is full of reasons to hope (see 3:15); his or her life is anchored in hope (see Heb. 6:19). But the hope found in the Scriptures is not only eternal life. As we've already seen, it is often the hope of revival. In fact, even the second coming of Christ—our "blessed hope" (Titus 2:13)—could be called the Final Revival from which every other passage on revival takes its cue.

God recently convinced me of this once and for all. Early in the morning day after day for almost nine months, I worked through my Bible from Genesis to Revelation. With a yellow highlighter pen, I accented every passage—stories, prophecies, promises, fulfillments of promises—that illustrates how God is the God of all hope, always ready to meet our desperate condition with a divine intervention that is "exceedingly abundantly beyond all that we ask or think, according to the power that works within us" (Eph. 3:20, *NKJV*).

When I finished my experiment, I was amazed that nearly half my Bible had turned yellow! This vision ignited into greater dimensions of hope in God. I have not retreated since. He is the source of "so much more," always ready to take us deeper, higher, farther.

Throughout the past 10 years I have watched millions of people rise up to proclaim this hope, to pray and prepare for nothing less than a massive spiritual awakening to Christ, beginning with each one of us. All of these people share a fundamental conviction: We have every reason to hope that God is willing and ready to impact our generation in answer to the united prayers of the saints; and to do so through an extraordinary outpouring of the Holy Spirit.

Even the secular press is picking up on this. Recently the *Wall Street Journal* ran an article by a leading economist at the University of Chicago titled "The Fourth Great Awakening," which predicted that national revival is the only hope for us on both spiritual and economic levels![1]

At about the same time *U.S. News & World Report* published a Billy Graham essay titled "Spiritual Awakening Comes to America" in which he said, "It is not too late.... It is my conviction that we are going to see a great spiritual renewal in America. Already evidences of it are apparent...."[2]

On the *NBC Nightly News,* Tom Brokaw did a five-minute "America In-Depth" report on the movement of prayer among high school students in our nation, actually allowing the viewer to listen in on teenagers praying for revival![3]

The cry for hope has never been greater. Virtually everywhere I travel, Christian leaders are admitting that clearly a Gap exists within the American Church—between what we are and what we could be. They are saying, "The great need of our people is to be revitalized with a renewed spirit of hope in God." And for good reason. Ominous signs are all around us.

Our nation is deeply torn over the role of religion in society. Spiritual pursuits are increasingly excluded from public life, while our troubled nation is beset by violent crime, broken families, deteriorating cities and racism. These realities are confirmed by the Index of Leading Cultural Indicators, which describes a society in the midst of seeming cultural demise—the vacuum of values.

Recent popular books suggest an air of cynicism and fear in many quarters: *The Coming Collapse of America, The Coming Economic Earthquake, The Coming Race War, The Coming Global Plague, The Coming Evangelical Crisis.* No wonder George Barna, a popular researcher of the evangelical movement in our nation, recently concluded that in the next 5 to 10 years America will experience one of two revolutions: anarchy or revival.[4]

What should be our response to the glaring Gaps, the spiritual decline in our country? In the words of James Dobson: "First, we must continue to pray for a worldwide revival that will re-awaken millions of people spiritually. This is not mere pious sentiment. Every great revival has been accompanied by social reform.... We seek the Lord in earnest prayer that He would once again grant revival to His Church in the United States and around the world."[5]

REASON FOR HOPE

One of the primary miracles that compels us to be prisoners of hope is the growth of prayer for revival throughout the whole Church. (Listed in chapters 1 and 6.) The *river* of revival may not be fully here yet, but the *feeder streams* are very active—more so than at any time in the history of the Church. As I asked earlier, if all these feeder streams are filling up the riverbed with the prayers of the saints, can the river of revival be very far ahead?

This prayer movement fills us with even greater hope when we stop to remember that prayer, all prayer, is a gift from God. Nothing in any of us naturally wants to seek God. No one naturally pursues the Holy Spirit to draw himself or herself into a more decisive devotion to Christ. And no one naturally seeks to unite with others in prayer across denominational and ethnic barriers...and then, to pray for revival (of all things)!

So the only explanation for this amazing prayer movement must be God. We can take heart in the principle of Philippians 1:6: "He who began a good work in you will bring it to completion at the day of Jesus Christ" (*RSV*). God has not stirred us up to pray in vain. He will not disappoint us.

Are you sensing this increased expectancy in the Body of Christ? If so, clearly, you are not alone. Worldwide, multitudes of Christian *men* are actively picking up the pace in the same direction. They are finally joining God's *women* in praying for spiritual awakening! (Although women make up about 60 percent of the Body of Christ worldwide, they represent 80 percent of the prayer warriors![6])

God is causing restless Christians to see a new day beyond the *status quo*—in their own lives, churches and communities—to challenge the idols of counterfeit hopes (where we have trusted in human resources, programs or experiences instead of Christ); and to fix their eyes on the biblical promise of a fresh encounter with the living Christ.

BROKENNESS IS THE HALLMARK OF ALL PRISONERS OF HOPE. IT IS THE SINGLE MOST IMPORTANT WAY TO GET READY FOR A GREATER WORK OF GOD.

Recently a group of us on America's National Prayer Committee produced a 30-minute video in which more than 50 national leaders comment on the prospects before our generation. The video's title says it all: *Get Ready—Christian Leaders Speak Out on the Coming Revival.* Prisoners of hope—every one of them!

As God increasingly impresses this hope upon us, we will become even more hungry for revival. The praying and preparing makes us hungry. The hope is at hand. Know that God wants revival for us far more than we want it for ourselves.

Feel a bit dry spiritually? God can raise you up even from a waterless pit and wrap you in hope. The second half of our study together will cover practical ways to grow as prisoners of hope, but for now, let's consider the basic qualification for believers who want to stand in the Gap, bringing hope to the hopeless.

BROKENNESS AND HOPE

Brokenness is the hallmark of all prisoners of hope. It is the single most important way to get ready for a greater work of God. It seems a paradox—that one who intends to stand strong in the Gap in the name of Jesus Christ must first be "weak" in his humility. But brokenness and hope are an unbeatable combination for those looking toward revival.

Repentance is based not so much on what we are turning from, but rather on what we are turning toward. "Repent and believe" was the message of Jesus based on the hope that "the time has come, the kingdom of God is near" (Mark 1:15). Repentance acts as a hinge that swings the Church *from what we are*—including all our sin and unbelief—*toward what is coming*, so that we make the necessary readjustments to receive God's reviving work in our lives.

Repentance is a heart broken with longing. Rather than just expressing regret over what could have been but never was, we long for what God has promised and is waiting to fulfill.

True brokenness relinquishes to God everything that revival must transform. Sometimes these may be good things. But God asks us to do more than simply let them go. He wants us to give them over to Him, to be transformed by the filling and outpouring of His Spirit.

As a person pursues brokenness, a desire to repent in the following areas will rise naturally out of his heart:

- Repent for choosing a lesser view of Christ, which has led you to a lesser concern for His purposes, presence and power.
- Repent for the unbelief that says your particular situation is hopeless and cannot be transformed, even by revival.
- Repent for attitudes of indifference and apathy. We are too willing to be satisfied with much less than what God has promised for us, and desires through us.
- Repent for "religious flesh." This is when we attempt to do God's work in our own strength. Religious flesh is evident in our self-sufficiency, self-confidence, self-righteousness and spiritual pride.
- Repent for counterfeit hopes centered on our own strategies and resources, on our churches and programs, or on particular Christian leaders and organizations—rather than on Christ alone.
- Repent for a lack of prayer as the Church. This reveals our hearts' hidden aversion to the living God and His kingdom purposes for all the earth.
- Repent for the disunity of the Church that makes it impos-

sible for God to pour out a broad-based spiritual awakening. God's whole work of revival must come to the whole Church, for the sake of the whole earth. We must repent of divisiveness caused by our denominationalism, traditionalism and competitiveness in ministry. But our brokenness will not be complete until we have dealt with our racism in the Church and the spirit of racial superiority.

- Repent for the "boxes" in your life keeping you from confident hope in God. Seek God's deliverance from past defeats and disappointments, or current spiritual weariness and fatigue, or fears of the future. In other words, pray daily for deliverance from sin and unbelief.

What would your life look like if you became bound up in hope? A prisoner of hope practices all the personal disciplines of typical biblical discipleship—which we will consider in the next chapter. But we can have a fresh perspective in those disciplines. We are not growing in Christ for our own sakes. We are growing so we can stand in the Gap—for fellow believers, for the nonChristians around us, for those who have never heard.

A TOUR OF THE GAP IN LOS ANGELES

Let's get practical about what standing in the Gap might mean. I'll illustrate the different widths of the Gap by taking you on an imaginary tour of Los Angeles. In early morning we head for the car.

My next-door neighbor, Mrs. Calley, waves a cheerful hello as she cuts roses from her garden. She is such a kind friend. I wonder how wide the Gap is for her? I'm not sure that she has ever come to a full faith in Christ although she has attended church for more than 30 years. My wife and I visited her fellowship with her one Sunday, and noticed her church's obvious desperate need for revival! (Mrs. Calley's church fits into the category Pastor Leith Anderson has warned about: Nearly 85 percent of the churches in America are either stagnant or dying!)

I wave back to Mrs. Calley, praying again that a genuine personal spiritual awakening would come to her heart and to her church. At the end of my prayer, as usual, I offer myself to God for anything He wants me to do to help fuel that revival, to close the Gap glaring within the American Church. I'm a prisoner of hope; it's as if I can't help but yearn for hope—that God would fill Mrs. Calley's life and her church with His.

Shall we go?

As our car rounds the corner, notice the rambling house on our left. The Pritchards hold a home Bible study there every Thursday evening. Most of the 45 people who attend haven't been in church for a long time, or go only on special occasions. But once a week they meet in this house to discuss the Bible as the Pritchards help them gain a fuller understanding of what salvation is all about.

For these people, the Gap is narrowing quickly. Before long they will be able to make an intelligent commitment to the Savior, and to perhaps begin attending the Pritchard's or another local church. Several already have made that commitment, and their new fire for Jesus is stirring up revival in their churches!

For two people a little farther up the street, however, the Gap is wider, and not much is happening to change the situation.

Across the street delivering the morning edition is our newspaper boy, George. Last week George told me he has never been in a church, never had a Christian friend and never read any part of the Bible. Basically, he doesn't know the first thing about the gospel. Oh, he's picked up a few things about Christianity. For example, he attended two voluntary assemblies at his high school this year when someone from Youth for Christ spoke about drugs and sex. He has also watched some evangelistic-type programs on late-night TV when he got bored with everything else. But the Gap seems seriously wide when compared, let's say, to Mrs. Calley's situation, and little is being done to narrow it for him.

In the park off to your right in this Anglo-American neighborhood, sleeping on a bench, is an immigrant from El Salvador. I've seen him there many times. Most people don't know his name. They just call him "the drunk." To my knowledge, he hasn't been completely sober for six years. During this time his family left him, he lost his job, his self-respect and any old friends who ever cared anything for him. What's the Gap like for him? Is there any hope?

Years ago as a child—I'm told by a local pastor—the drunk attended some backyard vacation Bible clubs. He even memorized enough verses to win a trip to a church camp where he learned to recite stories about Jesus. But as he grew older, school chums pulled him away from all that. Some time later he became a migrant worker with all the pressures and distractions this work entailed.

Long days in the fields left him little time to reflect on the stories of his Bible club days. When he lost his job, his tenuous financial world finally collapsed, the bottle became his only comfort. For years now he's been cut off from any compassionate help. Few Christians even notice that he exists; those who do, feel uneasy associating with him. Besides, his mind hasn't been in much shape to make decisions about Christ or anything else. His whole life is disintegrating while the Gap for him gets wider each day.

What are we going to do about the drunk? Let's take just a minute while I pop the trunk to get something I always carry around for the homeless. It's called a "Jesus Bag." Whenever we get together, my home fellowship makes up these sack lunches with nonperishable foods, a few clear tracts about Christ (some in Spanish) and a card with toll-free phone numbers for local ministries that can help the homeless with food, counseling and shelter.

Knowing God's heart for the poor and oppressed, the widow and orphan, we had better start praying for God's tactics to close the Gap for this man. And praying that I will be willing to stand in the Gap for him as God directs. Much as I hurt for him, even as a prisoner of hope I have trouble knowing how to penetrate his world with that hope.

Well, here we are on Interstate 10, on our way to the heart of the city. Let's stop briefly at the International Union on a local university campus. We've been invited to have coffee with some Middle Eastern students who just arrived in the United States this school term. As we sip and chat, you may be surprised at how easily we understand one another.

Not only do we all speak English, but their Westernized education before coming to the States makes them interested in many of the same topics we are. They are particularly interested in discussing religion and want to tell you about Islam, as well as listen respectfully to what you have to say about Christianity.

We are joined by some Christian students who arranged this meeting. Each student is a personal friend of one of the internationals. Each hopes to establish meaningful relationships which God can use to reach them for Christ. In fact, the Jordanians, the one from Iraq and the three from Saudi Arabia attend a dinner and Bible study that a Christian student group on campus sponsors once a month along with a group of older Christians from a nearby church.

What do you think the Gap is like around this table? In light of the geographical, cultural and theological changes taking place in the internationals' lives, the Gap which once was very wide continues to narrow.

In one sense, each international is now just *one person* removed from Jesus Christ—that one person being the Christian student who is becoming his or her good friend. That is a great leap from their families and friends back in Middle East towns and cities where the gospel has never been heard, where its preaching is forbidden, where people are so accustomed to living in spiritually waterless pits that solid hope never occurs to them.

Our visit is over. Let's head into Little Tokyo. On our way we'll take a swing through a well-known part of Los Angeles: Watts. What's happening with the gospel among the thousands in this African-American inner-city community? Who is spanning the Gap, for example, for the teenagers playing basketball down that street, or for those hanging around that corner bar? Who is going into those run-down government projects over there to reach disillusioned tenants with God's love? What opportunity do they *really* have to walk across the Gap to home?

Several years ago, I thought I had to jump into every Gap I encountered. I seriously considered moving into this area, as some Anglo Christians have done. If I were to make that move, the cultural and prejudicial distances between me and those I want to reach would not improve quickly. How long before I could be clearly understood with my message of hope? How much longer before they would even take the time or respect me enough to hear me out? How wide would I find the Gap here for me?

But now I know that God is always strategically positioning His prisoners of hope in the Gap. Sometimes that strategy is for me to stand as part of a *network*. I found that instead of living here myself and posing all those barriers, I was God-led to link up with African-American believers already living here. Praise God, a vibrant local church is located on the next block that has exploded in a fresh spiritual awakening, and as it links up with other revived churches of varying ethnic backgrounds, it is making a difference!

The church's pastor is approaching other pastors of Anglo, Asian and Hispanic churches across Los Angeles to pray for the city, to usher in the river of revival. Hundreds gather every three months for a half day of prayer they call "LOVE L.A." There *is* hope for the young people, the gangs, the neglected elderly and the lost of this community! And there's hope for my Anglo church as we are revitalized ourselves through all we receive from our African-American brothers and sisters beside whom we serve.

Well, here we are in Little Tokyo. One sight I especially want you to see—just behind that modern-looking Buddhist temple—is a tall apartment complex built for Japanese senior citizens. About a thousand live there now. Most of them are first generation Japanese; that is, they don't speak much English, they practice most of their cultural traditions and they are Buddhists.

I wish I could invite you in to meet some of them, but the guard at the door won't let us enter unless we are relatives or close friends with one of the tenants. Many of them are too sick to come out and talk, even if they could speak fluent English.

How wide is the Gap here? What opportunity do they have? Geographically isolated from most believers behind locked doors, culturally and linguistically distinct from most American Christians, and radically unlike any Christian in theology, they sit in their rooms, dying off one by one, just a 20-minute drive from my front doorstep. The Gap wouldn't be much wider if they lived in Tokyo itself! Who will bridge it for them? And how? And when? It is time for God to raise up prisoners of hope who won't turn away until the job is done.

We have time for one more stop before heading home. I'm leaving on a research assignment to India in a week, so I would like to pick up my airline tickets at the travel agent's office. As we move down the freeway to the other side of town, my thoughts bounce off the Los Angeles skyline. Here we live in a country with nearly 70 million people who claim to be born again. And yet even here the Gaps are intimidating. How insurmountable must be the challenge in people groups where few or even no believers exist at all!

I mull over the crisis-opportunity of the Gap that stretches out across this land, across the seas, across the villages and megacities of Latin America, Africa, Europe and Asia. In a week I will be on an express train from New Delhi to Madras. For 35 hours I will pass thousands of villages, and for every 1,000 villages I see, more than 950 will have absolutely no one to give them a clear witness about the Lord Jesus. In most cases, they won't even have heard His name. What hope do *they* have?

Imagine! A few hours of air travel will place me physically at the widest end of the Gap, a width that can be duplicated for more than a third of the world's population. Most of these men, women and children live in a neglected belt stretching from West Africa to the China Sea.

This block of humanity represents the poorest of the world's poor. They live in the homelands of the world's major nonChristian religions. And this part of the globe is the habitat of 95 percent of the unreached peoples of the earth. Recently this area, the widest part of the Gap, has been called "The 10/40 Window" because it lies between the 10 and 40 degree latitudes north of the equator. Prisoners of hope must pour into that window while there is time—and they *will*...recruited, empowered and sent out from the coming revival.

GET SERIOUS

Picture the people we have mentioned on our "tour." Try to visualize the billions more who are usually out of sight and thus out of mind across our neighborhoods and across our planet. As a prisoner of hope, you will feel increasingly uncomfortable about them. Thinking about them will hurt a little bit—maybe more than a little.

God has called you out of waterless pits. He has restored to you "twice as much" in Christ. He has recreated you to be captivated moment by moment with His promises for your generation. Will you stand in the Gap? Are you willing to be a prisoner of hope who almost has no choice but to bring the message of hope in Jesus Christ to your church, your community and your world?

Then get serious about a coming revival. And let me help you as we jump-start a whole new approach to your daily walk with Christ. Get ready to *thrive* in the Gap.

Notes

1. "The Fourth Great Awakening," *The Wall Street Journal* (January 9, 1996).
2. Billy Graham, "Spiritual Awakening Comes to America," *U.S. News & World Report* (December 24, 1995).
3. Tom Brokaw, "America In-Depth" on *NBC Nightly News,* September 16, 1995.
4. George Barna reported in *National and International Religion Report* 10, no. 7 (March 18, 1996): 1.
5. Dave Bryant, *The Hope at Hand: National & World Revival for the 21st Century* (Grand Rapids: Baker Books, 1995), p. 28.
6. Luis Bush, "Adopt-A-People Consultation Address," April 1994, Colorado Springs, Colorado.

5 | Standing in the Gap: The Call to Get Ready

Your Jump Start into a Daily Discipleship Wrapped Around God's Plan for the Nations

"I've been a Christian for 20 years," he said, "but I must admit that something is missing in my life. Can you tell me what it is? Can you tell me if there is something more?" There I sat in his living room, only two months into my first pastorate, with a great chance to do the things I had been prepared for. And I really bombed!

"Have you tried a private devotion time, Bill—you know, 15 minutes a day for Bible study and prayer?" Yes, he did that regularly. "Is any sin hidden in your life? For instance, are you a kind husband and father? Maybe you harbor bitterness toward someone." He was clean on all counts.

"Well, have you discovered the Spirit-filled life? What role does the Holy Spirit play in your walk with Christ?" His two-minute response told me he had the facts down straight and was truly seeking all God had for him in this area. As his pastor, I knew he attended church faithfully and tithed so I couldn't offer that solution. He did admit he was not the witness to his neighbors he ought to be, but he wanted to change this and was praying for them regularly.

So I read some Scripture with him, offered a brief prayer, promised to give it some more thought and walked away...into many similar sessions with other frustrated Christians until I finally learned what my friend was searching for.

Quite simply, despite all his good points, Bill lacked a cause. He needed something bigger than the issues we discussed that day to pull together everything else in his daily life and send it out to bless the ends of the earth. He needed to get beyond pea-sized Christianity, to *integrate* his Bible study, or prayer, or family life, or evangelism into a big-picture dimension. He needed a cause.

WHAT WOULD I SAY NEXT TIME?

I wish I had looked my friend straight in the eye and said, "Bill, I'll tell you what's missing. You need a cause to live for! Something bigger than personal spiritual maintenance or church activities. And you can have it! Focus your life in Christ on the whole world, nothing less, and you will have a cause on your hands! Discover that you don't have to be a spectator in God's global drama, but can become a teammate with those who are getting ready for serious spiritual awakening in the United States and across the globe, and you will have a cause on your hands. Let your discipleship overflow with a world-sized challenge and compassion, and you will have a cause on your hands, and your life will touch the ends of the earth.

"You don't have to think of your real life and then your Christian life as separate—because your 'Christian life' seems to revolve mostly around meetings and being nice. Beyond the people around you that you can touch, see, and care about, is the cry of a larger world: human beings with no personal knowledge of Christ, people God touches, sees, and deeply cares about. And, Bill, as you make that discovery you will find a cause that is really the 'something more' you're looking for. It will turn everything else you are and do as a Christian into an adventure without parallel!

"It strikes me that this was Jesus' point with the rich ruler who questioned him about eternal life. Let me paraphrase our Lord: 'After all your good and moral activities, you still lack one thing: You need my cause. Start by selling all you have so you are free to really reach out to those most neglected and most often unaware of God's love. Then, continue with my cause by following me only. I am on the move. You don't know it yet, but I am headed into a world full of physically and spiritually poor people. I am headed toward the ends of the earth!'"

Don't get me wrong. I would not tell Bill that the way out of pea-sized Christianity is simply to get *busier!* Rather, I would tell him that through a bold new faith that turns the sweep of world awakening into *the integrating factor* for all his other efforts at discipleship and evangelism, he will find a cause so compelling that he will have his "something more"—and more.

As past generations of disciples have had their place in God's ongoing plan, we too have been given a global cause for our moment in history. From the day you and I entered the Kingdom we have had Christ's cause as our high calling.

Jesus' summary of the cause is: "You will receive power when the Holy Spirit comes on you; and you will be my witnesses in Jerusalem, and in all Judea and Samaria, and to the ends of the earth" (Acts 1:8).

- Notice that the "you" and "on you" are plural. The cause is given to the whole Body of Christ and is fulfilled through them together.
- "The Holy Spirit" refers to the living God indwelling His people to unite us to Christ and to one another, to revive us, to transform us, and to lead us forth as Christ's ambassadors to transform our cultures and all nations.
- "Power" designates the Spirit's primary ministry in fulfilling the cause through us. He gives us ability, authority and effectiveness. His power means love without limits, both in how far it reaches and how fully it meets others' needs.
- "My witnesses" describes what happens when true revival hits: We have to tell someone about it! We bring other people to such a clear understanding of who Jesus is that they can render an intelligent verdict for (or against) Him. What a courtroom witness does for a judge and jury, we do for those who have never known Christ.
- "The ends of the earth" defines the cause as nothing less than global. The disciples were not to stop with seeing a personal awakening in their own hearts. As a Body, they would become messengers of hope to those near to them geographically, culturally and theologically—in Jerusalem. Some would go as an extension team to be agents of revival

in Samaria—with those relatively close at hand. And the Body would extend others to the ends of the earth—to those "who are far off" (Acts 2:39).

- "You shall receive power" and "you shall be my witnesses" remind us that Christ put rock-bottom stability into His challenge with this twofold promise. His promise gives us the right, in the words of William Carey's famous directive, not only to "*expect* great things from God," but also to "*attempt* great things for God."

Christ wants us to embrace a cause that will sweep to the ends of the earth before it is finished. This cause is the humanly overwhelming task of getting the whole Church ready for a massive spiritual awakening to Christ among the nations. No cause the world has ever known should be more consuming or more satisfying!

So maybe I've learned a few things since I was put on the spot as a young pastor. Maybe in the meantime I have caught the vision. If I could redo my conversation with Bill, I would conclude: "Bill, the discovery of this cause can end your search!"

Our lives as believers can seem incomplete because we are sectioned up like a *Time* magazine into a compartmentalized Christianity. Prayer does not seem to have much to do with ministry to the homeless; missions seems to compete with building programs. If our churches seem sluggish because they are fragmented into 12 equal but unrelated programs—then Acts 1:8 provides the new "cover" to bind up all those themes into the adventure for which we were made.

Christ only asks us to "staple" the whole thing together with our faith—faith working through love. Paul wrote to us:

> Above all these virtues put on love, which binds everything together in perfect harmony (Col. 3:14).

God's will for us can be put into a single word: *people*—the people *for* whom He wants us to give our lives and the people *with* whom He wants us to give our lives. We don't enhance our lives by trying to save our lives; we experience the fullness of salvation as we give. No wonder a central, God-ordered cause can jump-start our personal discipleship!

NOTHING COULD BE HEALTHIER

Living in a world dimension.... It all seems too big and difficult and complex to manage. There's too much stress to try to carry the weight of the world. And we might get hurt—or at least become uncomfortable. Couldn't we collapse as we try to prepare our whole nation and the world for a new Great Awakening? Is this cause truly *healthy* for practical day-to-day growth as Christ's disciples?

Yes.

We can remain healthy if we *simplify* the issues. For example, our great cause does not depend on us going at it alone. Even the apostle Paul never ventured out on his own. We are part of a movement of disciples from across our country and from many nations who can shoulder the cause together. We can relax. We can work on our own small but significant roles in the complex picture knowing that God sees it all and will effectively coordinate the efforts of His international team. We need not save the world by ourselves.

Furthermore, we can keep our sanity if we concentrate on one major cause at a time. We stand and God closes the Gap one step at a time—perhaps now strengthening our vision, perhaps next joining a prayer team focused on revival, perhaps in 10 years moving to the Gap's widest end in Brunei. (Find that one on a world map!) We are not doing things to fulfill God's worldwide purpose. He does that. We simply stand, for now, where He places us in the Gap. This is no Pollyanna cop-out on the world's myriad needs. It just keeps disciples sane to realize we can't "fix" everything...everywhere...all at once!

Conscientious Christians, faced with the modern evangelical smörgasbord, are crying out for a quality lifestyle of biblical discipleship that is simple, sane and yet significant. The single-minded focus of standing in the Gap just might be the answer.

One who stood for many years in the Gap in India, Donald McGavran, cautioned against seeking any other answer:

> As soon as we separate quality from the deepest passion of our Lord to seek and save the lost, it ceases to be *Christian* quality.... Even if we produce Christians who live as full brothers with men of other races but do not burn with

desire that those others may have eternal life, their "quality" is certainly in doubt.[1]

MORE DISCIPLESHIP MEETINGS?

What exactly is healthy discipleship anyway? It involves the gradual discipline of our characters until we become like the Savior. It also involves the growing development of our potential to glorify God. For those standing in the Gap full discipline and full development occur the more we get fully involved in the basic cause for which Christ came.

Didn't Jesus encourage this single-minded discipline and development when He summoned the Twelve to follow Him and learn to fish for others? He took them with Him into His own mission. Wasn't their

❖

A MATURE CHRISTIAN IS NOT ONE WHO PRACTICES THE RULES MORE. HE OR SHE IS ONE WHOSE DISCIPLINED LIVING HELPS HIM OR HER LOVE OTHERS BETTER AND FARTHER.

❖

quality of growth as disciples permanently affected as He helped them integrate and simplify their lives around the one cause of love in the Gap? So, 11 became healthy apostles ("sent ones"), sent out in His power to fish to the ends of the earth.

Practically speaking, healthy, quality discipleship involves learning to give away what we already have. We grow from point A to point B only as we first give away what we have received at point A.

The larger the giveaway, the greater the growth.

Discipleship is training someone to give better and farther. A mature Christian is not one who practices the rules more. He or she is one whose disciplined living helps him or her love others better and farther. Is this the kind of discipleship you are experiencing?

Let's look at the healthy changes the cause brings to the tried-and-true disciplines of discipleship: prayer, Bible study, purity, fellowship and outreach.

A HEALTHIER PRAYER LIFE

The cause provides a healthier perspective on what we pray about and the results we expect. God says through Ezekiel that one of the key factors in standing in the Gap is that we do it "before Me" or, literally, "before My face." We will explore this facet in chapter 10. For now, let's consider how prayer in general changes when it revolves around the big-picture cause of Christ.

This healthier dimension of prayer is illustrated in a prayer by the psalmist:

> God be gracious to us and bless us,
> And cause His face to shine upon us—
> That Thy way may be known on the earth,
> Thy salvation among all nations.
> (Ps. 67:1,2, *NASB*)

In this passage we learn that our personal requests—bless my family; strengthen the love in my small group; heal me of this disease; help me make the right decisions about a job; give me shelter from the cold winter; bring my best friend to Christ; and (quite urgently) revive Your Church again—should contain one overriding provision: "that Thy way may be known on the earth, Thy salvation among all nations" (v. 2, *NASB*).

When we articulate personal requests in keeping with an active concern for revealing God's name, Kingdom and will among all earth's people (the opening concerns of the Lord's Prayer), we are praying about the things God wants to do most. As a result, He will show us great answers!

When His answers to our prayers make an impact on blessing the world's peoples (never forgetting that our own ethnic group is one of those "nations"), then our praying will be truly effective. We will have asked for and received the right things. And we will be motivated to pray even more.

As we learn to pray beyond our own little worlds for people desperately needing spiritual life and for nations where darkness reigns and the evangelistic task remains so critical, we discover new vistas of faith for praying about our own needs as well.

What does this kind of powerful prayer look like? When George reads the daily paper, he prays over the front-page headlines. They remind him to pray for:

- Persecuted Christians in Asia;
- A Middle East summit meeting that might influence the future of missionary work;
- A local family devastated by the murder of a son;
- Indian Christians to have new opportunities to show Christ's love in the midst of the century's worst monsoon;
- A church other than his own that is reaching out to neighborhood kids in Good News Clubs.

Now, none of this has much to do personally with George. So his prayers are not skewed to what he wants (see James 4:3), but are firmly centered in what God wants. And God will answer his prayers!

Once a week three men who met each other at a Promise Keepers conference get together to pray. In keeping with their world vision, they always begin their prayer time praising God for His greatness and glory and His worldwide purpose in Christ. They praise Him for His great heart that yearns to bring new-life revival to whole nations.

They intercede for the needs at wider parts of the Gap—especially some people groups that remain unreached in the "10/40 Window" from West Africa to Japan. They plead for God to bring revival fire to the persecuted members of God's global family in Sudan, India and Indonesia. They gradually work their way back to concerns about America. Then they pray for their city, for the racial tensions in their neighborhoods and at their jobs, for reconciliation of factions in their churches. They pray for an outpouring of the Holy Spirit in their families and the Church families across our nation. And finally they pray about their own personal needs.

This approach puts their more immediate problems into perspective when compared with far greater tragedies and breakthroughs in the Gap. This kind of praying expands the scope of their concerns to the scope of God's concerns. And that is when prayer has power. (See 1 John 5:14,15.) It also provides them with a new faith about how God will answer their own needs as they learn to trust Him for bigger answers in the Gap.

A church in the East gathers every Saturday evening for prayer. They pray about personal and congregational needs, of course. But they basically divide their 90 minutes of prayer into two major segments. First: Prayer for revival in the Church, locally and worldwide. Next: Prayer for efforts to reach out in Jesus' name, locally and worldwide. As a result, many believe these prayer meetings are some of the most stimulating and life-changing they have ever been a part of. No wonder they keep coming back!

HEALTHIER BIBLE STUDY

The cause changes what we look for and what we find in our Bibles. Among other things, healthy Bible study will uncover perspectives and principles that not only lead to Christ, but also out to the world with Him.

Clearly, Bible study that turns into a spiritual sedative is not healthy. Instead, the Bible should stir up our faith in Christ's global cause, build our vision for a coming national and world revival, anchor our decisions to get actively involved and equip us to stand wherever the Gap needs us.

For example, as Sheldon has his devotions in Joshua, he looks for principles that God gave Israel for possessing the land. Every Saturday he plays pick-up basketball with street kids in an inner-city neighborhood of Chicago, and he is trusting God that the principles he is learning in Joshua will apply to "possessing" this block of Chicago for the cause of Christ.

Mary is memorizing some of the great promises of Isaiah. As she meditates on each one, she tries to picture how they could be fulfilled, not only in her own life but also in a far-reaching revival throughout America. But not stopping there, she also formulates fresh perspectives about the best outcome for conflicts among the Jews and Palestinians in Israel—the actual focus for the blessings described.

John's small group is studying Christ's Sermon on the Mount this quarter, but not merely as a devotional commentary. Rather, each verse helps to form their thinking about a strategy for a mission they face next summer. As a group they want to reach out to the Agul people of Dagestan near the Caspian Sea. And they want to be sure they reach out in the power of humility that Jesus prescribes in that Sermon. As they study, they are discovering much of the why, the how and the what for their mission.

On Sunday evenings First Church is enjoying a series that scans Paul's Epistles. Pastor White intends to help the congregation see that these are missionary letters written to churches Paul considered partners with him to reach the ends of the earth. Each week Pastor White illustrates this fact by suggesting ways the members can apply what they are learning to their own involvement to hasten a coming revival, to bless the nations.

Some First Church folks know their giftings are, right now, to strengthen the Church itself so it can move out in the cause. Others are glad that their "good works which God prepared beforehand [for them to do]" (Eph. 2:10) are impacting the poor of the city. Some are networking with other churches to bring searing renewal to the city's believers. And many are part of mission teams that are blessing other nations. Some of the team are out on the front lines; some of the team fill the backup support positions on the homefront. The lessons of the Epistles are consistently applicable because everybody is standing in some part of the Gap for the cause!

HEALTHIER MOTIVES FOR GODLINESS

When we discover that each of us is personally vital to a global cause for world redemption, our motives for staying morally pure begin to change. We find ourselves wanting to flee sin and pursue righteousness for more compelling reasons than just to remain trophies of moral spotlessness. Bitterness, greed, lust or pride cannot be tolerated any longer by those who want God to make their lives count significantly to usher in an historic Great Awakening.

The more we accept the fact that we are part of the hope for 3 billion unreached people, the more we crush our desire to sin, the more we understand that godliness gives support to the credibility and power of helping shape revival in the lives of more than a billion Christians worldwide, the more we will flee the traps of sin. As we accept our solemn privilege to help tell all peoples that Christ can cleanse the world's sin, we will *want* to be righteous like the Lamb of God who takes that sin away.

Paul was wrestling with a problem common to divorced men: His new dating relationships were riddled with sexual temptation. The old justifications that *giving in won't hurt anyone, no one will know,* and *God will forgive* almost miraculously disappeared when Paul met an Iranian international student one day at his fitness center.

Mohammed asked more and more questions about Jesus Christ and about the reputation for immorality that "Christian America" has in Muslim countries.

Paul realized that the eternal destiny of Mohammed and perhaps that of many of his family back in Teheran might depend upon a living demonstration of biblical moral purity. Because of that concern for the Persian nation for which Christ died, Paul resolutely and with surprising ease cleaned up his dating life. In fact, this new accountability for the sake of the cause makes his earlier justifications for immorality look juvenile.

We can be immoral about materialism, too, when we have no clear sense of lining up with God's big-picture purpose. Peter, a work-burdened marketing rep, found the more he learned about what God is doing in our world, the more he wanted to invest in a missions project. He chose a work among poverty-stricken migrant workers in Central California. Peter then realized that the more he sacrificially committed personal funds to this ministry, the less willing he was to falsely pad his expense account at work. Somehow that kind of "taking" couldn't coexist with his new-found "giving" in the Gap.

Allen and his wife wrestled with a different problem. They often argued. But as disciples growing in the Gap, they offered their home for weekly prayer sessions to plead for revival in their town. As Allen began to voice prayers for reconciliation in the neighborhood, as his wife pleaded for God to break through to a divorcing couple on their block, they realized their prayers would be hindered unless they themselves worked diligently on reconciling their own relationship. Christ's cause was too important to refuse to forgive, to fool around with petty bickering. Suddenly most of their old arguments did not seem so necessary after all.

A new hunger for personal godliness invades our lives when we take on the accountability to stand in the Gap. We no longer live unto ourselves.

A HEALTHIER LIFE TOGETHER

Missionary statesman Warren Webster once mentioned, "The spiritual vitality of any fellowship of Christians should be measured not simply by the number of believers it attracts, but by the number of disciples it sends out empowered for witness and service."

Such vitality can be found in many kinds of smaller groups. *Marriage*, for example, should result in the sending forth of two disciples newly equipped to close the Gap as "one flesh." Another kind of small group is *the family*. One family gradually cut its lifestyle back to the same standard of living as the missionary family in Kenya it helps support. Although the father makes $30,000 a year, they are living on $24,000 so they can free up $6,000 a year for those standing in the Gap for the unreached Massai people in Kenya.

The cause can also make for healthier small support groups in the local church, in the community and on campus.

Jesus and His disciples illustrated a healthy support group. They spent time together, communicated, studied, prayed, dealt with personal issues—and they also were active together in the Gap! In contrast, any support group that nurtures self-indulgence, vague commitments and isolation from a needy world is not healthy at all. Too many support groups are more like "retirement centers," where the members enjoy a weekly game of "Christian shuffleboard" as they shove a few Bible verses around and talk about their latest spiritual aches and pains.

With a global life-or-death cause before it, a support group won't settle for being just a collection of passive individuals. It will be a team on a mission that has integrated its caring and fellowship into the worldwide mission of Christ Himself. Fellowship and healing will be more the by-product of such a team rather than its purpose!

Larger gatherings of Christians grow healthier when the single vision of the cause is clear. In one church, for example, a large map of the world covers an area behind the platform. It indicates in brilliant orange dots where that fellowship is standing in the wider parts of the Gap. The map looms over the fellowship weekly as they seek God's face in hymns, liturgy and sermons. That way the members cannot forget the world as they look at Christ!

Most American churches fall easily into a pastoral mindset: *We are here to be taken care of.* But a huge number of the non-Western churches in the Body of Christ are more apostolic—a term suggesting "sending." These non-Western fellowships gather to worship, pray and learn *so they can be sent out*. And the nonWestern side of the global Body of Christ is reaping the harvest from that subtle shift of emphasis: Non-Western believers now represent more than two-thirds of the Body of Christ, and they are sending out more than three times the new missionaries than is the Church in the West![2]

One American church centering around the cause reports that in their whole-church gatherings, they seek to stress *sending* throughout a service by keeping the following four questions in mind regarding:

- *Celebration:* What has God recently accomplished in His global plan for revival and the blessing of the nations about which the congregation should praise Him?
- *Motivation:* What will encourage our people in this worship time to move on with their involvements in the Gap?
- *Training:* How can our people help each other improve their effectiveness to carry out their missions to the world?
- *Intercession:* What are the specific needs and opportunities for our church, for our nation and in our missions-to-the-world program that call for immediate prayer?

In small groups and large, let's face it: A clear vision of the cause will at least turn our meetings into meetings with a purpose! At best, it will fuel contagious spiritual growth, fellowship, edification and genuine worship.

HEALTHIER OUTREACH

Wherever you find people who make the Gap their life concern, you will discover their outreach expanding—where they are and beyond.

One middle-aged woman in Oklahoma concerned about the hungry and homeless in America is standing in the Gap. She is urging churches to link within a town or city to declare their community a "Hunger-Free Zone"! Others have caught her fervor, of course, and developed creative ways for gathering food to see that no one goes hungry in the name of Jesus Christ!

Racial reconciliation is becoming a familiar theme in the Promise Keepers rallies across the nation. And yet real reconciliation happens on a one-to-one level. Gap disciples grow to embrace the biblical fact that Jesus, who is our peace, has destroyed the barriers between races and ethnic groups—Jew and Gentile alike. (See Eph. 2:11-22.)

Recently in New York City, as a result of years of citywide Concerts of Prayer, nearly 200 pastors—the minority of them Anglo—met for a "Day of Reconciliation." Why? Because they believe God is answering their prayers; they sense revival is coming. They want to be ready to stand together for maximum outreach to the millions in the city, as God opens the way.

God leads some disciples to stand in the Gap of their cultures, speaking up on issues in behalf of Christ and His kingdom. He leads us in paths of righteousness "for his name's sake" (Ps. 23:3). A prisoner of hope, realizing God's reputation is at stake among the nations, will boldly step out against pornography, will bear criticism when promoting abstinence among teenagers, will vow to make a difference in the struggle over abortion.

And, obviously, a prisoner of hope is compelled to share his faith in Christ with others in his own culture in evangelism. Some prisoners of hope will also cross cultural barriers as missionaries—in relief and development, in church planting and church leadership training.

A commitment to the cause will expand outreach at the local level for a number of reasons. First, the challenge of billions of unreached people demands that outreach in general be given highest priority in our lives. Second, a global challenge demands that we learn to trust God's grace and power in new ways. And third, a passion for a coming national and world revival can't help but increase our confidence and boldness to reach out right where we live.

As we give our lives for the cause of Christ, all the disciplines of discipleship start to fit. The great theologian Elton Trueblood explains:

> A Christian is a person who confesses that, amidst the manifold and confusing voices heard in the world, there is one Voice which supremely wins his full assent, uniting all his powers, intellectual and emotional, into a single pattern of self-giving. That voice is Jesus Christ.... He believes in Him

with all his heart and strength and mind. Christ appears to the Christian as the one stable point or fulcrum in all the relativities of history. Once the Christian has made this primary commitment, he still has perplexities, but he begins to know the joy of being used for a mighty purpose by which his little life is dignified.[3]

Are you getting ready to be used for a mighty purpose? For the coming revival? Are you ready to stand in the Gap?

Notes

1. Donald McGavran, *Understanding Church Growth* (Grand Rapids: Wm. B. Eerdmans Publishing Co., 1990), p. 52.

2. Larry D. Pate, "The Changing Face of Global Mission," *Perspectives on the World Christian Movement: A Reader.* Editors Ralph D. Winter and Steven C. Hawthorne (Pasadena, Calif.: William Carey Library, 1992), pp. D229-D230.

3. Elton Trueblood, *Company of the Committed* (New York: Harper and Row Publishers, Inc., 1961), p. 23.

6 | So, Who Will Stand in the Gap?

You Were Brought to the Kingdom for Such a Time as This

⁑

"I looked for a man among them who would build up the wall and stand before me in the gap on behalf of the land" (Ezek. 22:30). God is looking for recruits to stand in the Gap. As any volunteer knows (Have you been asked to teach third-grade Sunday School lately?), it is a good idea to clarify the roles we are being asked to fill and the job descriptions.

Your Role in the Gap

We have been tossing around several terms that give a well-rounded sense of what God is calling us to in the Gap.

A *prisoner of hope* describes us as believers who know that we "once were lost, but now are found." The apostle Paul puts it in the following words:

> Since we have been justified through faith, we have peace with God through our Lord Jesus Christ, through whom we have gained access by faith into this grace in which we now stand. And we rejoice in the hope of the glory of God (Rom. 5:1,2).

As a *messenger of hope* we take this good news first to believers confined in boxes of pea-sized Christianity, in desperate need of a spiritual awakening to Christ; then on to those trapped as captives in darkness, those alienated from the God of all hope. Paul again puts it in a nutshell:

> For Christ's love compels us, because we are convinced that one died for all...that those who live should no longer live for themselves but for him who died for them and was raised again (2 Cor. 5:14,15).

As an *agent of revival* we stir believers to wake up, see the Gap and move out to take a stand in the cause of Christ. God urges us to be mobilizers:

> Let us hold unswervingly to the hope we profess, for he who promised is faithful. And let us consider how we may spur one another on towards love and good deeds. Let us not give up meeting together..., but let us encourage one another—and all the more as you see the Day approaching (Heb. 10:23-25).

As a *world Christian* we acknowledge that God has a heart for every people—not just Christians, not just Americans. A world Christian—a disciple with a global perspective—knows that the poor and the lost of every culture deserve to have someone stand in the Gap for them. Peter preached:

> [This] promise is for you and your children and for all who are far off—for all whom the Lord our God will call (Acts 2:39).

That's all about us. Now, what about the Gap? Let's summarize where we're being led to stand.

THE REASON FOR THE GAP

What is the Gap itself like? If you measure the Gap by the basic *reason* for it, you could say it is infinitely wide—because the reason for the Gap is sin. Sin and rebellion against a just and holy Creator have set us all the same distance from Him. Jesus measured it as somewhere between darkness and light, between the power of Satan and the power of God (see Acts 26:14-19). You can't get much farther apart than that!

In this sense, then, the Gap is the same width for everybody. Either you are an old creation in Adam or a new one in Christ; either you are dead or alive; either you are out of God's family or you are in it.

On one side of the Gap is a bundle of sins waiting for God's forgiveness; scars waiting for God's healing; needs waiting for God's riches; and potential waiting for God's power. From the other side has come the inexhaustible, yearning grace of God available in Jesus Christ to all of us in all the nations, with all the forgiveness, healing, riches and power the human race could ever want or need.

By this measurement the Gap is as wide as sin for everyone, but as crossable for all because the Son who forms the bridge is available for all. In one way, the Gap has already been closed for all because Christ has permanently stretched Himself across its chasm:

> When we were God's enemies, we were reconciled to [God] through the death of his Son (Rom. 5:10).

> For Christ died for sins once for all, the righteous for the unrighteous, to bring you to God (1 Pet. 3:18).

THE CHALLENGE OF THE GAP

One of the most interesting pictographs that make up the traditional Chinese alphabet is the character meaning "crisis." It combines two concepts: "danger" and "opportunity." The crisis of the Gap in our day similarly is a mix of both danger and opportunity. The danger of the Gap is explored in the context of Ezekiel's prophecies to God's people:

> The word of the Lord came to me: "Say to the land,... There is a conspiracy of her princes.... Her priests do violence to my law and profane my holy things;... Her officials within her are like wolves tearing their prey;...to make unjust gain. Her prophets whitewash these deeds for them by false visions.... The people of the land practice extortion and commit robbery; they oppress the poor and needy and

mistreat the alien, denying them justice.

"I looked for a man among them who would build up the wall and stand before me in the gap on behalf of the land...but I found none. So I will pour out my wrath on them and consume them with my fiery anger, bringing down on their own heads all they have done, declares the Sovereign Lord" (Ezek. 22:23-30).

Selah is one of those Old Testament words that suggests, "Pause and meditate." This disturbing context for standing in the Gap should cause us to pause and meditate on the danger of God's judgment falling on our country—on "both the righteous and the wicked" (Ezek.21:3,4).

Are we allowing corruption in the government of our land? Are ministers proclaiming sugar-coated, false "gospels"? Do we drink of the filth and violence that often spill out of Hollywood? Are we indifferent to the abortion of more than 4,000 unborn every day? Are the citizens of the United States oppressing the poor and needy? Is resentment and prejudice present among the races? Do we allow the mistreatment of noncitizen aliens? *Selah.*

If the Gap remains in the wall of God's protection and blessing around America, God will allow judgment to rush in through the breach. Dozens of good books are published and thousands of sermons are preached every year across our land that echo Ezekiel's warning. So we don't need to elaborate the dangers of not taking our stand in the Gap. We don't need to emphasize the gloom of *the alternative* to revival.

But the Gap is also a place of opportunity. As every business strategist knows, there is a flip side to dangers and problems. We are motivated to find new opportunities.

In Acts 1:8, Jesus talked about this other way of measuring the Gap as a *Gap of opportunity.* When He commissioned His disciples to stand in the Gap, He promised them that the Spirit's power would transform their lives so they could contribute directly to people's verdicts about Him: "You will be my witnesses" (Acts 1:8).

And He drew a map of the Gap that outlined the various widths they would face, the opportunities they would have to be messengers of hope, agents of revival. He spoke of "Jerusalem, Judea, Samaria and the ends of the earth." In other words, the Gap would vary in at least three ways: geographically, culturally and theologically.

The opportunity to come home to God would vary geographically for those on the other side of the Gap. Although Jerusalem and its surrounding territory, Judea, were important, the disciples would need to physically travel beyond there to Samaria in the north and eventually to the remotest areas of the Roman Empire lest these lands be forever isolated from the people of God and their witness.

We are to stand in the Gap in our own Jerusalems, offering hope to our neighbors, friends and coworkers. But our hometown is not to be the only geographical sphere of our concern. God will lead some to stand in the Gap in other places—perhaps in Timbuktu!

Second, the opportunity to come home would also vary *culturally* for those on the other side of the Gap. Regardless of where you stand in the Gap geographically, there will undoubtedly be both people who are like you and people who are not. If you live in Nashville, there are thousands from other cultures living across the Gap—hundreds of Kurdish and Bosnian Muslims, for example.

If you live within 50 miles of Times Square (as I do), you have around you hundreds of ethnic communities from virtually every major people group of the world. A passion to stand in the Gap against impending judgment upon America should not suggest that the message of hope is only for middle-class Anglo-Americans. The promise of a coming national revival is not just for one ethnic group.

Be sure your vow to stand in the Gap considers whether God would have you be the messenger of hope for a culture other than your own. If you live in Golden near Denver, the most powerful agents of revival may be the pastors of Hispanic churches there, messengers of hope to encourage Anglo- and African-American churches.

Standing in the Gap for another people group won't be easy, of course. For Jesus' first disciples, reaching the culturally different Samaritans meant the disciples would need to make special efforts to help them understand the message in a way that fit their own context. When it came to the "ends of the earth," the early disciples faced major cultural challenges. A message given to Jews in Palestine could be transferred to Cretan, Macedonians, Asians and Romans only as it came to these groups in relevant terms, using words and concepts that made sense to those the unredeemed Jew considered "unclean and uncircumcised dogs."

For some the opportunity to come home to God would be "near" *theologically* while for others it would be "far away." Jesus taught that "salvation is of the Jews." His message tied directly into the Scriptures and ceremonies that marked the covenant and its people. All that the Hebrews held so dear, revealed directly by God to His prophets, found its ultimate meaning in Christ Himself who transformed the covenant and made it new.

The Samaritans, on the other hand, were not quite so "theologically aware." Despite their reverence for the books of Moses and their worship of one God, they held prejudice toward many other covenant doctrines

##

MEASURED BY THE HUMAN CONDITION OF SIN, THE GAP IS THE SAME FOR ALL OF US. MEASURED BY THE DIVINE PROVISION OF A MEDIATOR, THE GAP COULD BE CLOSED FOR ALL OF US.

##

and had incorporated new ones of their own. Still the Gap was not that great. At the well of Sychar with Jesus and in Philip's preaching in Acts 8, we see a common ground of moral law and messianic expectations that allowed the good news to find spiritual affinity in the Samaritan soil.

For Gentiles, however, caught in the worship of Roman and Greek leities and with little or no exposure to the Old Testament, for whom a covenant-keeping Creator was "unknown" (see Acts 17:23), the Gap between a biblical witness and the Gentiles' own primitive understanding of God presented a major challenge. To give pagans and philosophers alike a just opportunity to cross this Gap forced the Early Church to face this complex need with clarity and relevance. Today's Church faces this in our mission to the 1 billion Muslims, or the 900 million Hindus or the millions in hardened post-Christian Europe.

Yes, there is a Gap. Measured by the human condition of sin, the Gap is the same for all of us. Measured by the divine provision of a Mediator, the Gap could be closed for all of us. But measured by the *human experience of opportunity* to know that the sin problem has been bridged, and to respond with faith in the mediator, the Gap differs widely around the globe.

Yet Jesus sent the disciples forth to serve in the Gap, regardless of its geographical, cultural or theological extremes. The disciples would have to tough it out in an eternally significant effort to see God reconcile lost sinners to Himself. They would be heralds of hope, bringing this message to every geographical corner of the earth, to every people group, to those both near and far from understanding God:

> Blessed is the nation whose God is the Lord.... From heaven the Lord looks down;... the eyes of the Lord are on those who fear him, on those whose hope is in his unfailing love.... We wait in hope for the Lord; he is our help and our shield. In him our hearts rejoice, for we trust in his holy name. May your unfailing love rest upon us, O Lord, even as we put our hope in you (Ps. 33:12-22).

Fortunately, throughout biblical history we have great models of prisoners of hope, of these agents of revival, of those who have stood in the Gap.

For example, God wanted someone to stand in the Gap between a great society turned sour and the new beginning He intended for the human race. So God called Noah to preach righteousness to his generation and build a craft that would take a remnant into the post-Flood world. Later, God wanted someone to stand in the Gap between His gracious resources for all nations and their fullest distribution everywhere. So He called Abraham and Sarah to leave their home, to go into a land of promise, to believe God could give them children in their old age and to receive the inheritance that would one day bless as many as the stars of heaven.

When God wanted someone to stand in the Gap between a nation of slaves and their deliverance, he called Moses to leave Egypt's comforts. Moses, Aaron and others led Israel into God's plan to make them a nation of priests, and as a result, directly changed the course of history for all peoples everywhere.

In one sense the entire Old Testament might be viewed as a series of case studies on different forms the Gap took through the centuries, and of those who responded to the call to stand in it, and what that stand meant for them.

But it wasn't just others God called to stand in the Gap. The mystery and majesty of our God is that ultimately He Himself stood there! Jesus forever became God's way home across the Gap. He fulfilled all the efforts of those who stood there before Him. He became the foundation for all the new efforts of those whom He drew forth to stand in the Gap with Him, to finish the reaching of the unreached in a way no Old Testament saint ever could or ever dreamed possible!

THE SON OF GOD IN THE GAP

Scripture is clear about the only One who actually can bridge the Gap: "For there is one God and one mediator between God and men, the man Christ Jesus" (1 Tim. 2:5).

For God, the Gap is a very personal issue. He has given the required Mediator to stand in the Gap forever, to close the distance between His own plan for world redemption and the consummation of that plan. He has given His own dear Son. He has a plan for the fullness of time, to unite all things in Christ, things in heaven and things on earth (see Eph. 1:10).

But more than that, the Mediator has actually *sacrificed His* own life in the Gap, falling like a seed into soil in order to bring forth fruit (see John 12:23-26), to bring many people home from the other side of the Gap.

That is why the Gap is a very personal issue for our heavenly Father; that is why He is personally concerned with the distance that remains between Christ's saving work and the impact of His Kingdom on people from every tongue and nation—our own included.

Like Columbus claiming the West Indies for Spain, Christ planted the staff of His cross in the middle of the Gap and flew the flag of His own broken body to reclaim this world for His Father. He is no "imperialist." He created the world, but He also *paid* for the world—all of it. His Kingdom is coming, in the Gap...at great cost.

Jesus the Mediator passed on His mission to His disciples. A major theme of the Gospels is: Jesus was progressively breaking His disciples out of the boxes that prevented them from believing they could effectively help close the Gap with Him.

During the last 40 days following His resurrection, the parallel passages of Luke 24:36-53 and Acts 1:1-8 tell us that Jesus concentrated on three areas of the disciples' faith:

- Their faith in His person—"everything written about me"; "many proofs";
- Their faith in His purpose—"that...forgiveness of sins should be preached in His name to all nations"; "be my witnesses to the end of the earth";
- Their faith in His promise—"you shall be my witnesses"; "you are clothed with power"; "you shall receive power when the Holy Spirit has come upon you."

Jesus knew that if the disciples' faith focused on these three truths, they would be free to stand in the Gap with Him and to close it. In fact, that is precisely what happened. Through them the gospel penetrated much of the first-century world. Initially, waves of revival rushed through communities of God's people at the narrow end of the Gap. Then came waves of revived believers evangelizing the Roman Empire and beyond—at the widest end of the Gap.

Today some Christians have the mistaken notion that when we are redeemed, we cross over the Gap between us and God and out of it to live safely ever after on the other side. But that is not altogether accurate. Jesus, in bringing us back to the Father, calls us to lose our lives with Him in this world, stating that "If anyone serves Me, let him follow Me; and where I am, there shall My servant also be" (John 12:26, *NASB*). Where is Jesus right now? In one sense, He is at the right hand of the Father's throne. But He is also active in the Gap!

And that's why the Gap is a very personal issue for us Christians today as well. The Gap lies between what God is doing in your life and mine—as people united forever to the Mediator—and what God still wants to do to bring revival and evangelize America and the nations.

Millions of us, for example, have asked the Savior to quench our thirst with His water of life (see John 7:37). But there remains a critical breakthrough needed in our lives; we call it revival. In revival, the living river that flows *into* the hearts of satisfied disciples leads toward the glorious day when it flows *out of* us to fully complete Habakkuk's vision:

> For the earth will be filled with the knowledge of the glory
> of the Lord, as the waters cover the sea (2:14).

That's why I say we Christians are right in the middle of the Gap. We have been born again for the sake of the Gap. Someday the waters of life are to cover the whole earth...through us.

But it won't be through our human efforts. The living Mediator remains the mediator! And the attitude that was in God's Son when He entered the Gap for our salvation is the same He wants for all His disciples (see Phil. 2:5-10). We're to stand with Him as He stood and stands there. According to 1 John 1:1, His approach to bridging the Gap wasn't the tossing out of an impersonal message. As it was through Him, the message of hope today must be:

- *Heard.* We are to speak good news so others understand it clearly.
- *Seen.* We are to be available to people, going to where they are.
- *Looked upon.* The message of hope is to be visible to those we want to reach as we are living models by which they can discover God's love for them.
- *Touched.* We are to be directly and personally involved in advocating among other believers the hope of revival, and in bridging the distance between God and specific unreached sinners somewhere in the world.

That all adds up to standing in the Gap. Paul understood this. He claimed to have been personally "appointed" to stand in the Gap (see 1 Tim. 2:7). According to his own testimony, that appointment came the very day He met Christ on the Damascus road. In that hour Jesus called him to "rise and stand" for a "purpose": to "serve and bear witness" not only among his own people but also with "the Gentiles—to whom I send you" (see Acts 26:12-23).

But then, Paul turns around and instructs all of us Christians to "be imitators of me, just as I also am of Christ...as I also please all men in all things, not seeking my own profit, but the profit of the many, that they may be saved." (1 Cor. 11:1, 10:33, *NASB*). Of course, we are not all called to be apostles. But like Paul, we should testify about the focus of our conversion:

> But when He who had set me apart, even from my mother's womb, and called me through His grace, was pleased to reveal His Son in me, [He did so] that I might preach Him among the Gentiles (Gal. 1:15,16, *NASB*).

God desires the whole Church to imitate Paul's sense of priority and purpose, each of us saying about our lifelong journey in the Gap: "I was not disobedient to the vision from heaven" (Acts 26:19). We can lie our heads down on our pillows at night with satisfaction that, *I know today my life has counted strategically for a God-given revival in my community and in my world.*

TWO IMPORTANT QUESTIONS

Now, will I *stand* in the Gap? That is, will I fully assume the privilege Christ has given me to be an agent of revival in my fellowship, and to bring the hope of the good news to my community and world?

A second question is of equal concern: In what *part* of the Gap will I stand? That is, what will be the width of the Gap where I serve Christ's cause? Who will blossom with the hope of revival because I laid out the promises so clearly for them? Who will pray and prepare for revival because I have led the way? At what geographical, cultural and theological distance from a clear witness to Christ are the ones I will reach with God's love? Who will have an opportunity to hear of Christ for the first time because I care?

God is looking for men and women to stand in the Gap. He is looking for people who believe the Gap exists, that Christ can close it and that they must be in it with Him. He is looking for people to walk in it with Christ, making a strategic impact for a spiritual awakening among all nations.

The man or woman God is looking for doesn't have to be in full-time ministry as clergy, a missionary, a full-time evangelist. No, He's simply looking for Christians who are willing to be changed, wherever that may lead. He wants disciples who will stand in the Gap humbly, knowing that what is wrong with the local church and with the world is also what is wrong with them, who are willing to be broken and remolded until they fit strategically in some needy part of the Gap as God chooses.

God is looking for the change I saw illustrated in India as I watched seven workmen rebuilding part of a collapsed stone wall. The wall had a hole in it that ran from top to bottom and about six feet wide. Their supply of stone to fill the hole came from some nearby boulders. First, they dynamited the boulders to break them down into chunks. Then they chiseled each chunk to form a stone that would fit perfectly in the next layer of the hole. Slowly the break was closed as one stone after another was fashioned and laid in its exact place.

Like a foundation stone Christ has been set in the Gap. No one else could ever be that rock. But God is looking now for "living stones" to be built on top of Him. He is preparing stones that He has broken and remolded to close the Gap as a "royal priesthood" that "you may declare the praises of him who called you out of darkness into his wonderful light" (1 Pet. 2:9). As a believer, you are part of that royal priesthood, and—as Queen Esther was charged—"Who knows but that you have come to royal position for such a time as this?" (Esther 4:14).

God has a place for disciples such as us who will allow our plans, gifts, jobs and abilities, schooling and training, our most intimate relationships and even our hopes for the future to be broken and remolded so our lives can count most strategically for the Kingdom—for now, and for the revival that *is* coming.

To stand in the Gap means to place no limits on how fully God may use you, or for whose sake. It means that, as God directs you, you are willing to take on any role, any time, any place, by any means, with anyone and at any cost that will help close the Gap, whether in an apathetic church or at its widest end.

So *who* will stand in the Gap? And *where* will he or she stand?

There is nothing ho-hum in all of this! It truly is an adventure. To stand in the Gap means to discover all that we are meant to be in this moment of history—to discover the cause for which God has placed us at this hour in His world.

PART II
Get Ready for the Coming World Revival

::

"Record the vision and inscribe it on tablets, that the one who reads it may run. For the vision is yet for the appointed time; it hastens toward the goal, and it will not fail."

—*Habakkuk 2:2,3* (NASB)

7 | Get Ready: Catch the Vision!

A World Full of Purpose and Possibilities

::

When the 40,000 pastors gathered in Atlanta's Georgia Dome for the National Clergy Conference in February 1996, they developed a statement to help clergy—and all prisoners of hope—become real agents of revival for the twenty-first century. In part it read:

> Our great and awesome God, in your sovereignty You have...met and dealt with us in powerful ways.... We now stand before You broken and humbled, called to shepherd and pastor Your Church, believing You are willing and ready to give a fresh outpouring of Your Holy Spirit on Your Church.... As You lead, we commit to fast and pray for the revival of our own hearts, for our churches, and for the Church of Jesus Christ.
>
> Where Your Church has lost its saltiness and light in our nation, we covenant to lead Your people to seek God's face for the healing of our land. Where we have lost Your vision to reach all people groups with Your amazing, saving grace, we covenant to freely give to others what You have given us.
>
> To that end, we give our lives as clergy to pray, to prepare and to minister for nothing less than a spiritual revival in Your Church.

Do you sense the anticipation? the urgency? the readiness? Have you discovered that this is what the Spirit is saying to all the churches right now?

Revival is coming. The nations are in view. It is time to get ready. In Part II, I want to share with you four key areas of preparation: Catch the Vision! Keep the Vision! Obey the vision! Pray the vision! To do this is to try to stand in the Gap. As you do, my prayer is that "you may abound in hope by the power of the Holy Spirit" (Rom. 15:13, *NKJV*).

A WORLD FULL OF PURPOSE AND POSSIBILITIES

First Key Question: Do I see the big picture of revival from God's point of view?

Fact: There *is* a worldwide purpose.

God's worldwide purpose is working its way out through history and among the nations. From Adam to Abraham to Israel to the exiles who returned to rebuild the Temple, that purpose was active but often channeled through one family, one clan or one tribe. But from Christ to the Twelve to the Early Church to Paul's missionary band and through the 2,000-year impact of the Christian movement, His worldwide purpose has flowed across the globe to thousands of people groups—including ours. That spread of the good news might be outlined as follows:

- *Penetrate* all human cultures with the reconciling gospel and power of Jesus Christ so as to...
- *Persuade* all kinds of peoples to become obedient disciples of Christ and responsible members of His Church where they live, so as to...
- *Project* into every society the redemptive alternatives of God's kingdom against the destructive forces of evil, so as to...
- *Press* the course of history toward the climactic return of the Lord Jesus to reign visibly over His victorious Kingdom, so as to...

- *Permeate* the whole earth with the knowledge of the glory of God as the waters cover the sea.

It is a purpose marked by *love*. In one sense God's purpose is the extension of the love shared eternally among the three Persons of the Godhead. That same love reaches out toward His lost children at every segment of the Gap.

> Turn to me and be saved, all you ends of the earth; for I am God, and there is no other. By myself I have sworn, my mouth has uttered in all integrity a word that will not be revoked: Before me every knee will bow; by me every tongue will swear. They will say of me, "In the Lord alone are righteousness and strength." All who have raged against him will come to him and be put to shame. But in the Lord all the descendants of Israel will be found right-eous and will exult (Isa. 45:22-25).

CHRIST: THE CENTER OF THE PURPOSE

Christ's coming is not one in a series of equally significant events in God's worldwide purpose. Rather it is the fulfillment event. He came in the fullness of times, giving ultimate meaning and direction to everything else God is doing among the nations.

As Abraham's nobler heir, Christ receives God's purpose to bless all earth's families and is Himself their guarantee. Through Him who takes away the sin of the whole world, God's purpose extends once and for all beyond one nation to the ends of the earth—beyond any one culture (Israel) to break through to all people everywhere. His blood can and will ransom sinners from every tongue, tribe and nation—our own included.

> In everything he might have the supremacy. For God was pleased to have all his fullness dwell in him, and through him to reconcile to himself all things, whether things on earth or things in heaven, by making peace through his blood, shed on the cross (Col. 1: 18-20).

Catch the vision!

THE NATIONS: THE TARGET OF THE PURPOSE

Christ's Body has become the most international society in the history of humankind. This should not surprise us. Almost every book of the Bible records something of God's intentions for and actions toward "the nations." Whether we look at the table of nations in Genesis 10 or the citizenship of the New Jerusalem in Revelation 21, we find that God's purpose has maintained one great target throughout: the world of the nations.

Even early on, when God summoned Abraham to come out from his kindred and be a part of His purpose, His summons was not for Abraham's sake alone. All the nations were summoned with him. God essentially said, "I will bless you so that you can bless the families of the earth" (see Gen. 12:1-3). All along God has intended to include people from every ethnic group and race in the inheritance of His dear Son.

Who are "the nations"? In the original Greek of the New Testament, "the nations" is *ta ethne*. *Ethne* is obviously where we get our English word *ethnic*. The biblical sense of the nations is not necessarily political countries. It's more the thousands of ethnic, cultural groupings around the world that make up the grand, creative, diverse community of humankind. Even in our own political country of America, we find hundreds of *nations* in the biblical sense—such as the Cherokee nation, the Cambodian Khmer nation, the Anglo nation.

Worldwide as many as perhaps 24,000 nations or *ethne* exist today, and about 10,000 of them have no strong Christian witness within their cultures.

God desires to declare His glory in the face of Jesus Christ within every one of these societies. He desires to reach them in ways expressive of who they are and in keeping with their own unique ways of experiencing His salvation.

No doubt about it: A day will come when at least some representatives from every tongue and tribe will be gathered before the throne in praise, to reflect like a grand mosaic the Father's glory through Christ Jesus, their Savior. And every piece of that human mosaic, once it has been penetrated and purified by the fire of the gospel, will make essential contributions to creating that spectacular display.

And they sang a new song: "You are worthy to take the scroll and to open its seals, because you were slain, and with your blood you purchased men for God from every tribe and language and people and nation" (Rev. 5:9).

Catch the vision!

THE GOSPEL: THE POWER OF THE PURPOSE

During this moment of history, God's kingdom demonstrates its presence and power through the impact of His good news in Jesus Christ, proclaimed by word and deed. God's great redemptive purpose expands throughout the earth as the gospel breaks through into individual lives and into whole societies—as it is properly understood, believed and obeyed.

Of course, the gospel never works in a spiritual vacuum. Wherever believers venture with the good news, God has prepared the way. Creation has set the stage for the message by testifying about God's presence and glory and goodness (see Rom. 1). Conscience has set the mood for this message by testifying to man's sin and guilt, and God's coming judgment (see Rom. 2). The convicting and convincing power of the Holy Spirit (see John 16) powerfully woos the lost.

But there is more. The gospel's power lies not only in its call to trust Christ for salvation, but also in its summons to believers to fulfill their destinies in Christ. It is good news not only about who Jesus is in us, but also what He will do through us.

The gospel invites us to both faith in Christ and a new life of concern for others for whom Christ died. He saves us not only for Himself, but also for His saving mission. Properly understood, the gospel should ignite a radical obedience that thrusts us out together to follow our Savior to the ends of the earth. "The gospel is God's power to save and send" (see Luke 24:45-48).

> I am under obligation both to Greeks and to barbarians, both to the wise and to the foolish.... For I am not ashamed of the gospel, for it is the power of God for salvation to everyone who believes, to the Jew first and also to the Greek. For in it the righteousness of God is revealed from faith to faith (Rom. 1:14,16,17, *NASB*).

The Spirit of the Lord God is upon me, because the Lord has anointed me to bring good news to the afflicted; He has sent me to bind up the brokenhearted, to proclaim liberty to the captives, and freedom to prisoners.... Then they will rebuild the ancient ruins, they will raise up the former devastations,

::

WE ARE TO BE MORE LIKE A CARAVAN OF AMBASSADORS GOING FORTH TO BLESS THE FAMILIES OF THE EARTH THAN A ROYAL ENTOURAGE BASKING IN THE SUNLIGHT OF GOD'S LOVE FOR US.

::

and they will repair the ruined cities, the desolations of many generations.... For as the earth brings forth its sprouts, and as a garden causes the things sown in it to spring up, so the Lord God will cause righteousness and praise to spring up before all the nations (Isa. 61:1,4,11, *NASB*).

Catch the vision!

GOD'S PEOPLE IN THE WORLD: THE STRATEGY OF THE PURPOSE

Righteousness and praise springing forth from every nation, of course, won't happen without a vital, revived global community of disciples who burn with the fire of a world vision. Christians are not meant to be a collection of spectators whom God asks to watch as He puts on a global extravaganza. We are not to sit by passively waiting for the Kingdom to suddenly materialize before our eyes.

The Church is the agent of God's worldwide purpose. We are to be more like a caravan of ambassadors going forth to bless the families of the earth than a royal entourage basking in the sunlight of God's love for us.

Some of us ambassadors bring our good news to the afflicted of our own people group through evangelism, or standing up for godly issues, or in community ministry where we give cups of cold water in Jesus' name. Some of us ambassadors venture across cultural lines to bring the message of hope to other "nations," other *ethne* whether within our own political country or in another.

But whenever believers step out beyond their own four walls as messengers of hope, they need to be part of a team, with some who go to the front lines and some who stay on the homefront as support personnel. For example, every cross-cultural missions team must have a mission movement behind it, a movement of local churches and Christians who pray and sacrifice.

God's strategy is to use His people to multiply. Once a church has been started in a people group, that congregation is potentially a time bomb, ready to explode into its circles of influence with Kingdom-style changes as new Christians grow and reach out to their friends and neighbors.

No matter how poor or talentless a local church may appear, that church is still God's base of operation within its locality. In that congregation dwells the living Christ in all His fullness. And out of His fullness these believers can penetrate their society with His grace and truth until the ultimate transformations emerge.

But what if a local church is not radiating into its surrounding culture? God is not willing to settle for a "token presence" in each of the world's 24,000 nations in its 220 political countries. He is not satisfied with a few sheaves of gathered wheat while ignoring the massive harvest still standing in the fields. *This is when God sends revival*, new vision and new resolve to stand in the Gap. New vigor comes to believers within the local church, which inevitably overflows into the neighborhoods, districts, regions and people groups around it.

The apostle Paul compliments the Church in Thessalonica for the "ripple effect" of its faith, love and hope:

> In spite of severe suffering, you welcomed the message with the joy given by the Holy Spirit. And so you became a model to all the believers in Macedonia and Achaia. The Lord's message rang out from you not only in Macedonia and Achaia—your faith in God has become known everywhere (1 Thess. 1:6-8).

Catch the vision!

CULTURAL TRANSFORMATION:
THE IMPACT OF THE PURPOSE

God's purpose will create an impact on both individuals and the community to which they belong. This will spring from the influence of faithful disciples whose living faith leads them to active, daily obedience where they are. Through the gospel, God incorporates new believers into local congregations where they learn obedience, experience personal liberation and engage in creative evangelism that liberates others in their society.

As these new and older, revived Christians live out their allegiance to Christ, they can accept, reject or transform what they find in their culture. And things change!

Every culture is full of treasures unique to it that have often been abused and misused for evil purposes, but that wait to shine with the glory of God. When Christ reaches and redeems people in a culture, there is much in that people which He desires to transform and place in His Father's house forever. What a day it will be when He will "shake the heavens and the earth" and "shake all nations, so that the treasures of all the nations shall come in [to fill this house]" (Hag. 2:6,7, RSV). Paul rejoiced with the believers in the city of Colosse:

> We always thank God, the Father of the Lord Jesus Christ, when we pray for you because we have heard of your faith in Christ Jesus and of the love you have for all the saints— the faith and love that spring from the hope that is stored up for you in heaven.... All over the world this gospel is bearing fruit and growing, just as it has been doing among you since the day you heard it (Col. 1:3-7).

Catch the vision!

SATAN: THE ENEMY OF THE PURPOSE

God has not abandoned our age to the powers of evil. But the Old Age is still hostile to any impact we prisoners of hope might have. We are engaged in constant spiritual warfare with Satan's hosts. Those willing to follow Christ into the Gap can't avoid the conflict of this age-long battle.

No territory is neutral. Among the nations God is at work calling citizens of the kingdom of darkness to a verdict about His dear Son through the gospel. Every advance into enemy-held territory (see Luke 4:5,6) can liberate some of Satan's captives. Accordingly, Satan's only alternative is to set himself against those most deeply involved in becoming messengers of hope, who are reaching out to those in Satan's grip within the Gap.

Sometimes Scripture describes this battlefield as the "world." Used in this way the term does not refer primarily to the physical world of nations, but to a system of organized evil put together by Satan himself to oppose the Kingdom's advance. This system might be organized as a form of nationalism, traditionalism, technocracy or military expansionism.

Or it may be expressed in the more obvious forms of idolatry, superstition and demonism. But in every instance, our real enemy remains the Evil One. Ultimately our battle is not against terrorism, racism or "human nature." Our battle is against the principalities and powers behind all these things, powers that exploit humanity in order to oppose God's worldwide purpose.

Of course, we need to be careful not to label every resistance to the gospel as satanic. Whenever the gospel is rejected or opposed, we must first ask: Are these people really opposed to Christ Himself? Or do they misunderstand my communication about Him? Is my economic status, ethnic background or "church culture" suspect? Are they reacting to my insensitivity or lack of evident love? In other words, is the problem with the hearer or with me, the speaker? Should I assume part of the responsibility for the problem rather than blame the devil?

But when we are faced with Satan's most threatening activities, we can always have hope. Actually, any onslaught of the opposition forces remains a clear indication of the even stronger advance of God's kingdom. Scripture teaches that evil is to increase concurrently with good as God's purpose in worldwide revival reaches its climax:

> And the great dragon was thrown down, that ancient serpent, who is called the Devil and Satan, the deceiver of the whole world—he was thrown down to the earth, and his

angels were thrown down with him.... And they [the saints] have conquered him by the blood of the Lamb and by the word of their testimony, for they loved not their lives even unto death (Rev. 12:9,11, *RSV*).

Catch the vision!

REVIVAL: THE ACCELERATION OF GOD'S PURPOSE

I am convinced that as we stand in the Gap we can look toward the hope of national and world revival for the twenty-first century. (I have written a whole book on this fact alone: *The Hope at Hand.*) And that revival will speed the culmination of God's historic purpose. This challenge of standing in the Gap brings not only a sense of urgency, but also a sense of eager joy.

The psalmist pleads, "Will you not revive us again, that your people may rejoice in you?" (Ps. 85:6). Unfortunately, some contemporary uses of the term *revival* smack of superficial emotionalism or images of programmed manipulated Christian zeal. To counter this misuse of the term, I usually talk about a "coming world revival" with personal, national and global ramifications.

By "world" I mean that the revival at hand is for the Body of Christ worldwide, not simply for a momentary period of congregational refreshment and renewal. The revival God wants to give His Church is not for our sake alone, but for the sake of many, many others—even for the blessing of all the peoples of the earth. God's promises of revival always have Christ's global cause in view.

By "coming" I mean revival is on its way! It is coming from outside our resources, our ingenuity and our control. Revival is something God must do, something God is bringing to us through His grace and the extraordinary work of the Spirit that invades the Church to reenergize us with God's eternal purposes in Christ Jesus.

Revival does not simply shape the future. To be sure it does help to do that as it unleashes the Church to press Christ's global cause on all fronts. But much more than that is involved. Revival is also a *receiving* of the future, of that which is the end of all things! In revival, Christ comes fresh to His Church, to conquer us in new ways that are truly precursors to the day when He will bring all things—the Church, the nations, history itself—under His feet.[1]

Catch the vision!

Second Key Question: Do I see the Church's potential for closing the Gap in my generation?

Fact: There *is* a world full of possibilities.

Almost 3 billion people have no opportunity to make an intelligent decision for Jesus Christ. But the world Christian, the prisoner of hope does not despair. We know that God is not finished yet. The Kingdom still comes! Throughout the earth God's purpose presses on, full and overflowing with possibilities for closing the Gap through His humble, obedient servants among the nations. The possibilities are as infinite as the God who gives them.

God is providing resources in the Church to bridge the Gap:

- Today more than 560 million worldwide are committed, active Christians.
- About 170 million of these pray daily for the hope of world evangelization.
- And every day, an average of 174,000 are added to the global Body of Christ![2]

Even if we look at the widest end of the Gap, where the world's remaining 10,000 unreached peoples live, we can catch an encouraging vision of the possibilities. An unreached people is one of the *ethne* or nations that has not yet been penetrated by a strong Church movement. These 10,000 naturally group into about 2,000 clusters comprising similar languages or cultural characteristics. Still, reaching 2,000 entire cultures with Christ's good news in the Gap seems intimidating. But not when we see the resources God has provided in His people.

Consider the ratio: Today about 7 million congregations of committed believers are ready to stand in the Gap for these 2,000 unreached clusters. That's 3,500 congregations of true messengers of hope per each unreached cluster! Could those 3,500 possibly pray, give and send several mission teams to that one unreached people group cluster? Even on a human level, the job of completing Christ's Great Commission to disciple the nations seems possible!

But we must be careful. A vision of possibilities—including past victories, present world trends, available personnel, money and resources—should never overshadow a key biblical principle: When we are weak then we are really strong because God's power is allowed full expression through our weakness (see 2 Cor. 12:9,10). The task before us should drive the Church daily to the Master in a sense of utter dependence. Our greatest "possibility" lies in our helplessness before Him.

But we also need eyes to see all the ways He has prepared to release His power once we rise from our knees to go forth.

Marked by its spiritual vitality, global diversity and available options, the Church has never been better equipped to close the Gap. The time has come to double our efforts. We stand on the threshold of a new era if we but believe and obey. Together we must mobilize to meet the possibility—or the probability—of the coming national and world revival.

CHURCH HISTORY POINTS TO THE POSSIBILITIES

We can see the potential for closing the Gap only if we look through dual-lensed spectacles. The biblical foundation for God's worldwide purpose prescribes the first lens. What He has said, He will do (see Isa. 38:7). When God said, "Be still and know that I am God; I will be exalted among the nations, I will be exalted in the earth" (Ps. 46:10), He meant it. We can expect Him to provide opportunities for us to fulfill our role in His global purpose.

Church history prescribes the second lens for glimpsing the possibilities of our experiencing a coming world revival. The more we know of the Spirit's accomplishments throughout the centuries (beyond Acts 28), through Christians from all parts of the world, the more we will be reinforced to believe in great possibilities today. No other movement has so dramatically changed the face of the world and the course of history.

Unfortunately, many of us have succumbed to the BO-BO theory of Church history (a term coined by Ralph Winter). This theory postulates that the Spirit has "Blinked-On" (BO) and "Blinked-Off" (BO). Throughout the past 2,000 years, so the theory goes, He has often "Blinked-

Off"—at least that's what our personal perspective suggests to us. Mistakenly, we look at the familiar high points of Paul, Luther, Moody and John XXIII and assume that in between God has been "off"; He has not been too involved. (After all, they *were* the Dark Ages, weren't they?)

If this were the kind of God we served, we could be excused for shifting uncomfortably when someone talks about a coming revival that could shake our nation and the whole world. Maybe God is about ready to blink off again. Maybe for good.

However, another theory is needed to explain a movement that is 83 million times as large as when it began in A.D. 31. In those early days of Christianity, there were 360 unbelievers to every true believer in Jesus Christ. Today there are less than 7 unbelievers to every true believer![3]

Obviously, God's love has been relentless. We have compelling reasons for hope.

Catch the vision!

TODAY'S PRAYER MOVEMENTS POINT TO POSSIBILITIES

Throughout Church history, prayer movements consistently preceded major outpourings of God's Spirit. Today, the burgeoning prayer movement in the United States alone suggests great possibilities for a new spiritual awakening in the Gap:

Every year now tens of thousands of Christians from thousands of churches and hundreds of denominations are uniting in mass prayer rallies in cities across the continent. Hundreds of thousands of others are joined on a daily basis by radio broadcasts that lead the nation in prayer. In addition, toll-free numbers and the internet offer immediate access to information about the rapidly growing prayer movement and about the ways God is answering with preliminary phases of revival.

Twenty-eight thousand Canadian Christians recently met in a sports stadium for a "Save the Nation" prayer rally, claiming the promise of 2 Chronicles 7:14. This prayer gathering was sponsored by 300 churches and coupled with an evangelistic outreach afterward.

In some cities traffic jams have occurred at the locations of mass prayer rallies because so many Christians showed up to the prayer meetings. In one rally people literally had to be turned away from the prayer meeting at the largest auditorium in the city because no more seats or parking places were available.

Groups of 70 pastors each gathered in four different cities (in four regions of the nation) during the same week to pray for nationwide revival. Most of the groups prayed and fasted for 24 hours or longer. No one in any of the groups knew that similar pastors' gatherings were taking place simultaneously elsewhere. This is part of a growing phenomenon of pastors' prayer gatherings in many cities.

In 1993, 300 leaders, from 166 denominations and Christian ministries, from 35 states, representing almost half of the protestant churches of North America, gathered for a National Consultation on United Prayer, issuing a national call to united prayer as a result. A few weeks later a three-day National Prayer Summit took place in Canada with 200 leaders from across the nation. A National Prayer Summit in the United States has called for a gathering of 600 leaders to spend four days of "prayer only" for revival in the nation.

In the Pacific Northwest only 3 percent of the population claims any church membership. And yet, during recent months as many as 3,000 from nearly 100 different communities have gathered together for Prayer Summits in this part of the nation. These Prayer Summits involved 30 to 40 pastors from a single community, spending four days of intercession for one another and for their cities.

In one such gathering, several African-American pastors actually "commissioned" Anglo pastors to preach the hope of revival, a hope already alive in many African-American churches. These Anglo pastors have returned to mobilize the churches into citywide concerted prayer and have successfully mobilized nearly 100,000 in united prayer within a short time. (See Joe Aldrich's *Prayer Summits: Seeking God's Agenda for Your Community,* Portland: Multnomah Press, 1992.)

An estimated 800,000 Americans marched in more than 300 cities throughout all 50 states in a "traveling prayer movement" called Marches for Jesus. In places such as Pittsburgh some 40,000 marchers turned out on the day of the march to stand in the Gap with praise and prayer for their cities and for the nations.

A significant groundswell of prayer among high school students is being registered in a number of ways. National conferences are taking place, involving thousands of high school students who come together for three days of nothing but prayer for revival on their own campuses and others throughout the nation.

Every September for the last several years, students have gathered in early morning prayer groups around the flagpoles on tens of thousands of high school campuses to begin the school year interceding for revival on their campuses.

More than 3 million students gathered at the most recent "See You at the Pole" event. These gatherings have resulted in thousands of ongoing prayer groups throughout the year in an effort called "Locker 2 Locker." More than 10,000 student-led Bible studies are now occurring on the campuses of public schools in the United States.

Recently a nationwide evangelistic outreach to high schools through television was preceded by weeks of prayer concerts inaugurated and led by high school students in cities from coast to coast. As a result an estimated 75,000 students made commitments to Christ on the night of the evangelistic outreach—one of the largest responses ever among high school students in a single evangelistic event.

A similar movement is occurring among college students. At one university on the West Coast, 300 to 500 students meet every week to pray for revival. At a major student mission conference involving nearly 20,000, an entire night was recently devoted to intercession for the worldwide advance of the Kingdom. And college students have sponsored grassroots regional conferences to pray and train together for mobilizing for revival on their campuses.

For the last few years America's National Day of Prayer has seen a tremendous increase in the participation of millions of Americans who take the first Thursday of May to intercede for our country. These dedicated believers have done so through morning prayer breakfasts, evening Concerts of Prayer, 24-hour prayer watches in churches and prayer rallies at city halls.

Recently tens of thousands gathered at municipal buildings to pray for America in more than 2,500 locations. And on the evening of the National Day of Prayer, literally millions of Christians have been united by thousands of radio and TV stations in a three-hour "live" Concert of Prayer that has united the Church in revival from coast to coast.

A number of denominations have devoted their annual denominational meetings to explore a denominationwide call to united prayer for revival. In a number of cases a "year of prayer for revival" has resulted.

Currently within one denomination, "solemn assemblies" are taking place within individual congregations and among congregations within specific regions. At the same time thousands of churches have been linked in a prayer watch that covers every hour of every day and night of the entire year with prayer by intercessory groups within one or more churches.

Another denomination that sought to mobilize 1,000 retired pastors to give one hour a day in prayer for revival have found themselves overwhelmed with commitments by some 5,000 pastors.

Members of an urban church that grew from 500 to 5,000 in just five years recently shut down all church activities with the exception of Sunday morning worship to give themselves for a period of weeks to pray for revival. Every night for eight weeks they saw thousands of their people coming together in prayer.

In another city a Lutheran church has taken on a full-time pastor of prayer and has seen 2,000 of their members turning out once a week for united prayer. Many churches are experiencing similar enthusiastic responses.

In New England a prayer movement is growing on many levels in a five-state area. Several rallies have attracted thousands of participants in this region of the country that is one of the least churched.

In another city 300 churches have formed an ongoing prayer movement focused on praying for revival throughout the Christian community to achieve a strategic impact on hundreds of thousands of international visitors who will be involved in international sporting events within their city during a four-year period.

In another city a movement of hundreds of women in prayer has adopted 1,000 of that city's pastors, so each one is prayed for daily by at least two intercessors.

In an underevangelized city on the East Coast, a prayer movement developed, primarily by pastoral leadership from scores of African-American churches, with a focused consensus that if they would build a citywide prayer movement, God would pour out revival on the whole city. This movement was also directly linked with a mass evangelistic outreach.

In New York City, hundreds of churches are pulling together for a "Lord's Watch" (see Isa. 62:6,7). Every hour of every day and night of the year is covered by one or more churches with intercession for spiritual awakening. The assigned churches for each night pass the torch along to the groups for the next night by a phone call of report and encouragement.

Church leaders in one of America's largest cities have scheduled specific weekends for Concerts of Prayer in 10 or more different regions of the city simultaneously. These have involved thousands of people being led by hundreds of pastors from all kinds of denominational and ethnic backgrounds.

In one of the most dangerous sections of a major city, hundreds of pastors took the "risk" of gathering together in a church that was guarded by armed police in order to spend a half day interceding for revival in that section of the city as well as in the whole city.

One citywide prayer movement made up of 300 churches has set its sights on a seven-year commitment, involving both pastors' prayer gatherings and citywide prayer rallies as well as local church prayer gatherings to pray unrelentingly until revival comes.

A prayer movement in a large city in the Midwest that has been brewing for almost nine years has now broken forth into 6,000- to 7,000-person prayer rallies, involving more than 300 congregations, plus rallies involving thousands of teenagers. All of this is focused on prayer for revival. And all of it is impacting the lives of pastors and local congregations on an ongoing basis.

In a recent prayer rally in the Midwest, the participating pastors were invited to come forward for specific prayer for themselves, for their ministries and for revival in their congregations. As 200 walked to the front, the audience of 5,000 gave them a standing ovation and then extended their hands in prayer for God to bring spiritual renewal to each one.

In Southern California as many as 1,000 pastors at a time have gathered quarterly for three to four hours of united prayer for revival in their cities. They have also assembled their churches in prayer rallies of as many as 10,000. When urban race riots occurred, about 700 area pastors who had been united in this movement joined in prayer and ministry in the aftermath of the riots.

Lloyd Ogilvie of Hollywood Presbyterian said, "Being part of this prayer movement has been a profoundly moving experience. The separateness, aloneness and self-gratifying independence have been replaced by honest sharing of our needs, penetrating prayer for one another and unified, shared discipleship and mission in our city."

Dr. Benjamin F. Reid, a respected African-American pastor, said, "One of the greatest spiritual blessings to occur in our community is this movement of prayer. God initiated this interracial, cross-cultural, inter-church prayer gathering. And the Holy Spirit has honored it. I see it as a major spiritual force for good in the future as we continue to glorify Christ and to intercede for the deep spiritual needs of our city."[4]

God is moving in our day, and the possibilities for us to get in on His plan are exciting. But the possible opportunities aren't just *options:* To whom much is given, much is required. And we believers in the United States have been given much.

Global researcher Patrick Johnstone once remarked, "Much of the burden for world evangelization rests on believers in the United States of America—about 63 percent of all missionaries and 90 percent of all funds."

Campus Crusade for Christ at one time estimated that 80 percent of the world's trained Christians and 70 percent of the evangelical church's material resources can be found in the United States. The fact of this reservoir holds great promise for impacting the cultures in our own country as well as the world wherever its supply is released through humble, responsible prisoners of hope!

Surveying this reservoir of resources, Gordon-Conwell historian Richard Lovelace said, "One cannot help but wonder what the result would be if the mass of laypeople [in American churches] could be spiritually released from their servitude in the American success system and reoriented to channel their major energies toward building the kingdom of God."[5]

Of course, if a widespread release of manpower, prayer power and finances were to sweep the American Church, the accompanying revival would probably spur an intensification of persecution. That should be expected, for Satan cannot remain idle and people cannot remain neutral when the Kingdom expands. Yet the attacks we suffer will only intensify the renewal as the Church is driven to a total dependency upon Christ for further evangelizing power. The Church's weakness is always its greatest opportunity to be renewed for God's purpose because it is compelled to pray:

> "Lord, look upon their threats, and grant to thy servants to speak thy word with all boldness, while thou stretchest out thy hand...." And when they had prayed, the place in which they were gathered together was shaken; and they were all filled with the Holy Spirit and spoke the word of God with boldness (Acts 4:29-31, *RSV*).

Catch the vision of God's purpose—and of the possibilities He is providing for us to stand in the Gap. And get ready to keep the vision—to make it *your own!*

Notes

1. David Bryant, *The Hope at Hand* (Grand Rapids: Baker Books, 1995), adapted from pp. 44-50.
2. Bob Sjögren, Bill Stearns and Amy Stearns, *Run with the Vision* (Minneapolis: Bethany House, 1995), pp. 23-24.
3. *Mission Frontiers Bulletin* of the U.S. Center for World Mission (May-August 1996): 3.
4. David Bryant, *The Hope at Hand*, pp. 231-237.
5. Richard Lovelace, *Dynamics of Spiritual Life: An Evangelical Theology of Renewal* (InterVarsity Press, 1979), p. 151.

8 | GET READY: KEEP THE VISION!

STANDING IN THE GAP WITH HEART, WITH OTHERS, WITH A PLAN

As you consider *keeping* the vision of a grand spiritual awakening in the Gap, ponder the following fable.

Once upon a time there stood a startling geographical wonder: The Mountain, they called it. How gorgeous it was! So royal!

The Mountain ruled over the snug little valley below where thousands of local citizens went about their daily tasks—watering lawns, driving trucks, writing term papers, eating Big Macs, selling shoes and playing games of soccer.

Every once in a while, however, the citizens just *had* to look up and draw in a glimpse of the towering peak. How it made their spirits soar! Looking at The Mountain made living seem more grand, more majestic—even during their everyday routines.

But a mysterious spell hung over the valley. Periodically, a brownish mist (evidently some witch's brew) shrouded it unmercifully. And because the valley had no outlet, the hovering mist had the power to actually make The Mountain disappear! It might vanish for a week at a time.

During these disappearances, the valley citizens' horizon rose no higher than the tallest office building. And The Mountain climbers in the foothills simply got lost. Nothing seemed to go right without that refreshing, exhilarating vision of the peerless peak. Truly a sad state of affairs.

But lo! The spell worked another ghastly ill. The trucker, the student, the shoe salesman, the climber—everyone, in fact—was forced to cough and wheeze as they trudged through their routines. Many people cowered indoors, barely daring to breathe.

The valley residents cursed the potion, calling it "smog." The smog left them stumbling in the haze. It suffocated them. There seemed to be no relief, except to cry out, "Curses on that wicked witch!"

::

BOXED-UP SPIRITUALITY TURNS STALE FAST, NO OUTLET MEANS NO UPLIFT!

::

And so it is that every generation of Christ's disciples faces the threat of a similarly dim, suffocating haze. Whenever Christians turn away from a Kingdom-style vision of Christ and His global cause, things soon end up like the air trapped in the valley basin. We become small minded, self-centered, picky, divided and lost. History bears us witness: Boxed-up spirituality turns stale fast. No outlet means no uplift!

Under this spell, Christians have trouble with their vision:

- God's big-picture purpose looks foggy and vague.
- We just do not see the possibilities for life-changing revival.
- A world full of people without any knowledge of Christ is out of sight, out of mind.
- Focusing on a personal part in something as big as the Gap becomes difficult.

What's more, under this spell Christians eventually *suffocate* because they are:

- Unable to keep and share a clear vision of all that Christ's cause should mean to them;
- Unable to become rescue teams sent out into the canyons

of their valleys and the world beyond as messengers of hope to those trapped and dying there;

- Unable to resuscitate asphyxiated disciples, giving them a revived vision of where Christ is going and of how they can go forth with Him in the Gap.

Back to the fable...

One day the ancient west winds began to blow with great force. The winds were boundless, breaking the spell! They washed the smog from the valley, restored sparkle to The Mountain and oxygen to the citizens. Again the stars studded the night sky and the robins returned to sing. Everyone rejoiced. And throughout The Mountain's ravines the trapped and dying were rescued. What a glad, glad ending!

Similarly, Christians can escape the sorcery of self-centeredness. Like a mighty wind, the Spirit of God can reverse the introverted patterns in our discipleship. He can uncover for us a crystal-clear view of God's majestic horizons—Christ's global cause. He can inject the grandeur of eternity into all our efforts down in the valley, wherever God places us and whatever He assigns us to do. He can fill the lungs of our souls with His breath, so we will have the strength and vitality to bind up the wounds of the afflicted, bring reconciliation and rescue the perishing everywhere.

God's holy wind can free us to move out, breathing deeply and seeing clearly. No blindness. No gasping. Revived. Awakened. We are released to be all we were meant to be...standing in the Gap.

Is this a vision you want to *keep*?

MY PART IN THE VISION

It's one thing to *catch* a clear vision of God's purpose and the possibilities in the Gap. It's another thing to make that vision your own, to keep the vision. How does that happen?

First, we face a crucial question and acknowledge a life-changing fact.

Key Question: Do I believe that I, along with other Christians, can have a strategic impact on the coming revival and all it will do for Christ's global cause?

Fact: There *is* a world-sized part for me.

A frequently quoted "law" among evangelical Christians claims: "God loves you and has a wonderful plan for your life." It's true that my loving Father wants to be very personal with me as He leads me into His perfect will. But if His plan for me ever becomes divorced from His plan for the nations, then I will lose the fundamental basis for a personally significant role in the Kingdom's advance in my nation and in the world.

The familiar adage might better be: "God has a wonderful plan for my nation and all the earth—and He loves me enough to give me a strategic part in that plan!"

MY PART IS WITH CHRIST—"FOLLOW ME" (MARK 8:34)

All Christians have been conscripted by Christ to go with Him into the Gap. To all of us who have made peace with the Father by Christ's cross, our Lord's very next words are: "Come. Follow me."

So the vision of our part of the cause depends not so much on who we are, why we believe we are here or where we are going. Rather it depends on *who Christ is,* why *He* is here, and *where He is going*—because we are following Him. Believers never journey into the Gap alone. Christ and His purpose create the larger dimension to our lives because our part is with Him. He has chosen us to join Him but never to launch out ahead of Him. He alone leads the way.

Jesus is on the move. And He wants us to follow Him out across the borders of our own world—beyond our familiar routines and comfortable friendships to spread hope across the street, across town and perhaps across the cultural borders of our own social and cultural securities.

MY PART IS TO LOSE MY LIFE—AND FIND IT!
(MATT. 16:25)

As faithful stewards of all we have received in Christ, we are directed by Christ Himself to actively invest our lives for the greatest possible returns in impacting our world. Ultimately that investment is in *people.*

Losing ourselves for Christ's cause—denying ourselves and taking up the cross—is the greatest love we can ever show the world. Our world-sized part is not fulfilled simply by being involved in outreach activities and revival events, but in love that fully invests our all in people. The person may be the neighborhood convenience-store clerk, or a relative or a Laotian Buddhist you have never met. We are to reach out to these people in the name of Christ no matter what it costs to do so.

No sacrifice that a lover would make for the beloved is too great for us to make in order that the earth's lost might be wed to our Savior. We are called into a world-sized part that asks us to be willing to even die if that will help bring them into the reality of God's greater love for them.

With Christ we are serving a Kingdom that will remain forever because *it is built of people.* When you've found out that people are worth dying for, then you've found something worth living for. So we always live whenever we invest ourselves in Christ's cause and His good news for the sake of people. (See Mark 8:34,35.)

In the context of Christ's global cause, what does it mean to *find life?* Just as our Savior did, we should give our flesh for the life of the world—we should stand in the Gap for those for whom He died. But that's not the end of it! As His blood opened the way of reconciliation, so our investment in His cause, no matter how costly, has its returns also. We help harvest those who are reconciled from among the nations. We share with Him in bringing new sons and daughters into God's family. We help fill the Kingdom with people who will praise our Lord forever. They will be forever our "crown of rejoicing" (1 Thess. 2:19,20, *NKJV*)! And all that adds up to finding *real life.*

Fulfilling a world-sized part points us beyond knowing ourselves, purifying ourselves or improving ourselves. Christ calls us to *multiply* ourselves! Miracles big enough to change the world, big enough to penetrate peoples where the gospel has never gone before, can happen through any who follow Christ and lose their lives for His sake and the gospel's. God wants to use finite, often fallible Christians to unleash His reviving work in our churches and upon the very ends of the earth.

It is no coincidence that the same century that has seen more people become Christians and more churches planted than in the previous 1,900 years put together, may also have seen more believers martyred for Christ worldwide than throughout the rest of Church history combined. The best research reports that an average of 135,000 each year are presently martyred for their faith in Christ![1]

Of course, those reports usually happen in far-off places and are rarely reported on the news. The nations are finding life because so many were willing to die for Christ's sake and the gospel's.

All of this indicates that we are actually participants in Christ's cause rather than just puppets in it. Though we may represent little or nothing in ourselves, we have become strategic "somebodies" who make a life-or-death difference for individuals and whole nations because we serve the King of life. In one sense, the fate of the world rests in the hands of nameless but committed saints through whom eternal life is multiplied.

The apostle Paul found plenty of life in the Thessalonians as he multiplied himself through them:

> For our gospel came to you not only in word, but also in power and in the Holy Spirit with full conviction.... And you became imitators of us and of the Lord, for you received the word in much affliction, with joy inspired by the Holy Spirit; so that you became an example to all the believers in Macedonia and Achaia. For not only has the word of the Lord sounded forth from you in Macedonia and Achaia,...but your faith in God has gone forth everywhere (1 Thess. 1:5-8, RSV).

MY PART NEEDS THE HOLY SPIRIT (ACTS 1:8)

Our world-sized part with Christ is a theological fact of Scripture and a daily experience developed through the Holy Spirit. The Spirit has come to make our world-sized part as defined in Mark 8:34,35—following, losing and finding—a permanent, daily event that brings a world-sized blessing.

Our part in spiritual revival is always complemented by His part through us. As the Spirit led and empowered Christ's own earthly mission—in words and miracles, in confrontations with Satan, in sensitivity to the Father's will, all the way to the cross and out of the tomb—He continues to do so for all who follow the Lamb. As we open to His forward-looking power, as we cast aside our fears of change, the Spirit will be to us all that He was to Christ.

Whenever Christians give top priority to standing in the Gap for others, the Spirit has His greatest freedom in our lives. He is free to produce His fruit in us, and transform our characters to make us more like the One whose mission we are on. He is free to build the Body up in love, to unify us into a family with a focus. He is free to develop in us the skills and abilities He has given us to effectively serve the cause. In summary, the Spirit is free to bring new life into the Gap when He has ambassadors of Christ whom He has changed, unified and equipped for that very calling.

No wonder a familiar phrase used in past Great Awakenings to describe what God was up to was "outpouring of the Holy Spirit." Without Him neither revival nor the fruits of revival are possible. We cannot do it ourselves!

The world-sized impact of Paul's stand in the Gap was directly attributable to the Spirit:

> When I came to you, brethren, I did not come proclaiming to you the testimony of God in lofty words or wisdom. For I decided to know nothing among you except Jesus Christ and him crucified. And I was with you in weakness and in much fear and trembling; and my speech and my message were not in plausible words of wisdom, but in demonstration of the Spirit and power, that your faith might not rest in the wisdom of men but in the power of God (1 Cor. 2:1-5, RSV).

MY PART NEEDS THE WHOLE BODY (EPH. 4:1-16)

At its deepest level, God's family can be defined by its mission. Jesus Himself stated that those who do the will of His Father are His brothers and sisters. Doing the ultimate will of the Father for this generation—hastening spiritual awakenings to Christ—is what His family's life on earth is ultimately about.

Within this family are many ministries, but only one mission. Within this family is beautiful diversity, but God intends it to be "unity in diversity" because we are united in the same cause. Each of our world-sized parts are interdependent and indispensable for our overall mission. The gifts and resources in the Body, both locally and globally, are there to make the Body strong and life-giving to the world beyond itself that needs to know our Head.

What's exciting in our day is that the diverse, squabbling members of the family are coming together. We are granted the "ministry of reconciliation" (2 Cor. 5:18) in the Gap. But before we can offer our giftings for the cause, if our brothers or sisters in God's family have anything against us, Scripture is clear: "First go and be reconciled to your brother" (Matt. 5:24).

John Dawson, founder of the International Reconciliation Coalition in Southern California, notes:

> As the Church of Jesus Christ, our goal, of course, has always been to see people reconciled to God through the gospel. The main hindrance to this end, however, has been *us*. The world has not been able to "see" Jesus because of the sectarian strife within the Body of Christ.
>
> For centuries, the spirit of religious controversy has made us part of the problem. But now, I believe, we are finally becoming part of the answer. The growing wave of repentance over historic sins is leading believers of differing denominations, cultures and movements to unprecedented affection and respect for one another. Jesus said that when this kind of unity occurred, the world would believe the Father sent Him (see John 17:21). Ultimately, the world will "see" Jesus when a united Church carries the ministry of reconciliation beyond its own walls....
>
> God has always looked for intercessors to repair the breaches and stand in the Gap. If we have broken our covenants with God and violated our relationships with one another, the path to reconciliation must begin with individual acts of confession.[2]

Worldwide, the various parts of the Body of Christ are responding to the Spirit's initiative to confess, repent, reconcile and restore relationships. New Zealanders of European origin and the native Maori have embraced each other in reconciliation ceremonies.

Japanese and Korean pastors have asked each other's forgiveness for atrocities in past wars. An historic Reconciliation Walk was launched in 1996 along the routes of the Crusades to ask forgiveness of Muslims, Eastern Orthodox and Jews for the Crusaders' slaughtering of their ancestors.

Here in the United States of America, the need for reconciliation among churches and between ethnic groups is obvious. A song raised in hundreds of recent Promise Keepers rallies cries, "Let this be the generation of reconciliation."

⊞

FAMILY UNITY IS NOT UNIFORMITY....
OUR DIVERSITY IS OUR STRENGTH.

⊞

As Raleigh Washington observes: "When revival comes—and it is coming—it will wear the face of reconciliation."

Family unity is not uniformity, however. Our diversity is our strength. We can maintain our distinctives, traditions and preferences. And we can honor the various streams of the Church. God allows us to be different parts in the Body. But if someone is a true believer in Jesus Christ, he or she must scripturally seek the unity of the Spirit: "Make every effort to keep the unity of the Spirit through the bond of peace" (Eph. 4:3ff). We can stand in cooperation in the Gap.

This shoulder-to-shoulder standing in the Gap is not a theoretical ideal. It is practical. Whatever we come to call ourselves as we keep the vision—whether an agent of revival, a prisoner or messenger of hope, or a world Christian—we were not meant to be lone rangers. Even the great apostle Paul never ventured out by himself without a team.

When we add our individual part to a team, we demonstrate God's synergy. In 1 Cor. 3:9, the words "fellow workers" are, in the original Greek, *sunergos*, from which we get "synergy." Synergy means the whole is greater than the sum of its parts; your stand becomes stronger when you stand with others than when you stand alone. Together, we can become "world Christian fellowships" or "revival teams" in our communities. The gospel permeates lives and societies best through disciplined, organized groups of believers who are constantly reaching out.

The New Testament Church "turned the world upside down" through its small teams of in-the-Gap believers. Consider some of the people on Paul's team:

> Paul, Silvanus, and Timothy, to the church of the Thessalonians.... We were ready to share with you not only the gospel of God but also our own selves (1 Thess. 1:1; 2:8, *RSV*).

> I have sent [Tychicus] to you for this very purpose, that you may know how we are...and with him Onesimus, the faithful and beloved brother, who is one of yourselves.... Aristarchus my fellow prisoner greets you, and Mark the cousin of Barnabas...and Jesus who is called Justus.... Epaphras, who is one of yourselves, a servant of Christ Jesus, greets you, always remembering you earnestly in his prayers.... Luke the beloved physician and Demas greet you (Col. 4:8-14, *RSV*).

THE DECISION

To keep your part of the vision in God's historic purpose and to make it your own, you will need to face a three-fold decision:

- Will I choose to *stand* in the Gap?
- Will I choose to *join with others* in the Gap?
- Will I *plan* to obey this vision?

All three issues are interlinked. One decision implies the other two, because none can ever survive by itself. All three together constitute the *second* step in the journey of standing in the Gap: Your decision to *keep* a vision of personal, national and world revival at the center of your life in Christ.

One of the great leaders of the Student Volunteer Movement and the Laymen's Missionary Movement in the early part of the twentieth century was John R. Mott. He recognized the need for every Christian to face this decision:

> Without a doubt there comes to many of us the choice between a life of contraction or one of expansion; a life of

small dimensions or one of widening horizons and larger visions and plans; a life of self-satisfaction and self-seeking or one of unselfish and truly Christlike sharing.

To keep a world vision for revival at the center of your life in Christ is no small step. But you can't really take the step until you've caught a sense of what that vision entails.

Have you *caught* the vision? In the following review of what we have studied so far, put a check mark beside the facts about which you feel confident, to which you can respond: "Yes! I see that! I accept that! I know it's important. I want that area to enlarge my relationship with Christ and to strengthen my commitment to His cause."

_____ As one who is hatching, I must break out of my shell.

_____ A Gap exists in American churches—between who we are and who we can be once we are fully awakened to all Christ is for us, in us and through us.

_____ There is a Sin Gap between people and God that is bridged in Jesus Christ.

_____ Unless someone stands in the Gap in our society, God's judgment will ultimately break through upon America.

_____ The widest part of the Gap is in the unreached people groups of the world—especially in the "10/40 Window" from West Africa to Japan.

_____ Great Awakenings have happened before; God is able, willing and ready to do it again.

_____ We *need* personal, national and world revival.

_____ Perhaps the greatest Gap of all is the Gap of Unbelief in Christians such as I.

_____ God is making us into "prisoners of hope"—so captivated by the hope of His purpose that we feel compelled to become "agents of revival."

_____ Moving out into the Gap is healthy for my prayer life because I am not focused on myself.

_____ Standing in the Gap is healthy for my Bible study because I am not focused on myself.

_____ Deciding to be an "agent of revival" is healthy for my moral stand because I am accountable for the spiritual destiny of others.

____ Being a "world Christian" is healthy for my church and small group because we prioritize God's great purpose over our own agendas.

____ Standing in the Gap makes my personal outreach healthier because it sharpens how I share the hope within me.

____ Following Jesus into the Gap integrates or pulls together all the disciplines of my discipleship into a single vision.

____ There is a worldwide purpose in Christ.

____ Christ is the center.

____ The nations including ours are the target.

____ The gospel is the power.

____ God's people are the strategy.

____ Cultural transformation is the impact.

____ Satan is the enemy.

____ Revival is the acceleration of God's purpose.

____ A world full of possibilities is available through Christ to see that purpose fulfilled.

____ Church history points us to a wealth of possibilities based on what God has done before.

____ Today's global prayer movements point to the possibilities because this is where all revival begins.

____ I, along with other Christians, can have a strategic impact on the coming revival and all it will do for Christ's global cause.

____ There is a world-sized part for me in what God is doing to bring spiritual awakening in the Gap if I:

    ____ lose my life for Christ in the Gap—and find it!;

    ____ follow Christ in the Gap wherever He takes me;

    ____ allow the Holy Spirit to empower me;

    ____ team up with the Body of Christ to stand in the Gap together.

In other words, do you see the following areas well enough to prepare you to *act* on them?

____ The big picture of Christ's global cause to close the Gap.

____ The Church's potential for fulfilling that cause.

____ The need for revival to release the Church's potential.
____ The strategic impact you can have as an individual.

If your answer is yes, you're ready to decide to *keep the vision.* (If not, this is a good time to review *Stand in the Gap* chapter by chapter!)

Pray—really pray—about signing the following statements:

STANDING IN THE GAP

I have caught a vision of the coming revival and its impact for Christ's global cause, and I want to be ready. This means I acknowledge that:

1. God has a worldwide *PURPOSE* in Christ that encompasses all history, all creation and all peoples everywhere—here and to the ends of the earth.
2. A world full of *POSSIBILITIES* is available through Christ to significantly advance that purpose in our generation through widespread revival.
3. God has given all Christians a strategic *PART* with Christ that can make an impact in my church, my community, my nation and in the unreached peoples of the world.

Therefore, I choose to keep this vision of hope. I choose to:

- *Stand in the Gap,* unifying my whole relationship with Christ around His cause.
- *Join with other believers* as we team up to get ready for a coming national and world revival.
- *Plan my obedience* to this vision around four areas:

1. *Build* my vision regularly about the coming revival.
2. *Share* this vision with other Christians, leading them to be prisoners of hope with me.
3. *Fulfill* the vision as I reach out directly to the world in love.
4. *Pray* the vision back to God every step of the way.

Signature _____ Date _____

That's the essence of *keeping* a vision of hope. But let me clarify two points:

Join with Others

What does this entail? Simply this: You have decidedly caught the vision when you choose to join other activist Christians who also want to *keep* the vision.

Believers who are stretching their hearts and nerves and strength and resources to care about closing the Gap *must* have people around them who share that same vision. We must remain accountable to one another if we are going to realistically get ready for a coming spiritual awakening. This is the only way obedience to that vision can last the strain of involvement. That's why a decision to stand in the Gap must include a decision to be part of a team. (List your possible accountability partners.)

Make Plans to Obey Your Vision

What does this entail? It means you'll *organize* your efforts for Christ's global cause. Most believers who stand in the Gap do this around the following essential components:

- Regularly *build your* vision.
- *Give* your vision to other Christians.
- Fulfill your vision as you *reach out* in love.
- Get good at *praying* your vision before God.

This is a crossroads. You must *plan* for obedience in the Gap. You must believe that God has specific ways He wants to involve you, and that His Spirit will help you develop specific plans to fulfill that calling.

What plan of action could you follow? Jot down some ideas.

I have a growing vision of revival, of serving Christ in the Gap. I want to wrap my life around the cause of Christ. As I do this, I expect to see important changes in my day-to-day life in the following selection of areas (Describe one possible change you could make in each area.):

- My daily Bible study:
- My daily prayer life:

- Activities with my family:
- My involvement in a small group:
- Use of financial resources:
- Praying and reaching out in my neighborhood:
- Involvement in my local church:
- My plans for the future:
- My life on the job:
- My involvement in the political process:
- Other:

Who is one person I could approach to grow with me as a kind of accountability partner—a fellow prisoner of hope—as we stand in the Gap together and get ready for coming revival? (List possible names.)

Notes

1. David Barrett and Todd Johnson, *Our Globe and How to Reach It* (Birmingham: New Hope Publishing, 1990), p. 21.
2. John Dawson, "Blessed Are the Peacemakers," *Ministries Today*, (Jan./Feb. 1997): 22.

9 | GET READY: OBEY THE VISION!

STANDING IN THE GAP AS
YOU WORK YOUR PLAN

∷

I'm sure you have heard about the race car driver who entered the Indianapolis 500 for his first big professional race. He was nervous. His courage almost won him the race, but the grueling pace caused him to fall back and he finally came in second. Why? Because he had to make five unscheduled pit stops: two for gas and three for directions! (Think about it.) In the same way we don't want to go racing around in the Gap unprepared, lacking direction and the stamina needed to live for a coming revival.

Rather than jumping recklessly into action, we need to carefully build our vision. Otherwise we might just be running on zeal—"but not according to knowledge" (Rom. 10:2, *NKJV*).

Visionaries are usually enthusiastic zealots. But as any poor soul who has struggled to develop an effective business plan knows, ideas and visions are the easy part. More difficult is the practical outworking of that vision in realistic objectives and action steps.

How do we obey a vision to stand in the Gap? We make it practical for day-to-day life.

The vision of the Promise Keepers movement, for example, has been distilled into seven practical commitments. A Promise Keeper commits himself to honor Jesus Christ, develop relationships with a few other men, practice purity, build a strong marriage and family, support his church, reach across racial barriers and be obedient to the Great Commandment and the Great Commission.[1]

Obviously a believer observing these commitments would be standing in the Gap in behalf of his church, his culture and the ends of the earth. But what would the tactical, daily steps look like as a believer *obeys* promises such as these?

FIRST, BUILD THE VISION

Key Question: Will I take time to study the cause? Will I let my vision for the coming revival grow?

God usually does not lead us on the basis of facts we do not have. So to get ready for a coming revival in the Gap, you will need to *intentionally* schedule into your week time slots when you will focus on strengthening your vision.

A "quick-start" list of ideas for building your vision might include:

- Reread and mark key points in this book, jotting questions about the hope of revival that you will study later.
- Highlight Bible passages that reflect the extraordinary kind of hope God gives His people.
- Read a great book about the Great Awakenings of the past, such as Wesley Duell's *Revival Fires* or Robert Coleman's *The Coming World Revival.* (See Resources.) Check your church library or local Christian bookstore for these and other titles.
- Consistently pray the message of hope back to God. Pray God's Word of hope into your life and the lives of those around you. Praise Him for every sign of revival you already see.
- Reshape your prayers to begin with God and the great scope of His Kingdom and talk about yourself only toward the end of your conversations with Him. He is infinitely interested in you and wants to hear you pray about your own needs. But *you* need to hear yourself pray about your own needs in the true context of the cause!

- Refocus your daily walk with Christ, so the disciplines of your discipleship—Bible study, prayer, etc.—are not stuck in the what's-in-it-for-me mode, but focused on what *God* is doing. Consistently expect and prepare for revival in your own local and Christ's global church.
- If you have succumbed to fearful defensiveness and "gloom-and-doom" expectations, constantly work to revise your thinking. "Take captive every thought to make it obedient to Christ" (2 Cor. 10:5). Forcefully climb out of the Gap of Unbelief. God is the one who says, "Call to me and I will answer you and tell you great and unsearchable things you do not know" (Jer. 33:3).

That's the quick-start program. But reliable, accurate visions are not built with quick-fix lists. Consider what you will do in the following suggestions to build your vision:

BECOME ACCOUNTABLE

1. *Tell your church pastor* or other leadership that you intend to be a believer who "stands in the Gap" and ask for prayer. You don't have to try to explain all the implications of this, you certainly shouldn't simply announce that you have been "called to missions" or whatever. For your own sense of accountability and the encouragement of your church leadership, tell them God is doing something in your life, filling you with new hope and that you want to faithfully respond.

2. *Enlist prayer partners.* Usually the elderly, and usually the elderly women, of a fellowship have the heart, experience and time to genuinely pray. Ask two or three of these prayer warriors to pray for you in your journey of discipleship in the Gap. Pass on your personal prayer requests and praises to them regularly.

3. *Find an accountability partner.* This is a person who will hold you accountable for the disciplines of discipleship, who will ask you the impolite questions such as:

- Is there any unconfessed sin in your life right now?
- Are you spending time in the Word?
- Are you spending time in prayer?
- Are you consistent about the commitments you have made?

This person may be a close friend who gets together with you to study and work through this in-the-Gap journey. Or it may be a mature Christian who even at a distance will ask you those tough questions. Keep yourself accountable.

If your explorations of your part in the Gap suggest God is leading you into cross-cultural ministry, connect with The LOOP, a guidance system for those wanting to send or be one of the twenty-first century's new missionaries. The LOOP suggests key steps for your accountability, awareness and preparation with no cost or obligation. It is operated by several "generic" ministries and sends LOOPers back into their own church's mission efforts. Get into The LOOP of the information (resources, opportunities and information) about what God is doing globally by calling The LOOP at (800) 388-9915.

STUDY

Work steadily through what you can learn about:

- God's grand purpose;
- The possibilities of what He is doing globally among the nations and locally among your own people;
- Your part in the Gap.

Where do you find the resources for these studies? First, in the Resource section at the close of this book. Second, by connecting with those who are resources themselves. The following are some suggestions:

- Order videos and books from Concerts of Prayer International.
- Become a member of World Christian, an association of global activists who provide a key interactive newsletter, electronic access to global information, seminars, conferences and expeditions in the Gap.

- Attend gatherings: a Promise Keepers rally or local PK breakfast, an Aglow International function, a National Network of Youth Ministries session, a National Prayer and Fasting Convocation, etc. Any group that meets to pray and strategize to stand in the Gap will coach you into further insights about God's purpose, the possibilities and your part.
- Enroll in a *Perspectives on the World Christian Movement* course in your area, at a Bible college, seminar or by correspondence. Contact the Perspectives Study Office for information (Phone 818-398-2125).
- Find someone in your fellowship who is comfortable with accessing the WorldWide Web on the Internet. Search the Web for key sites such as Goshen with its Religion News Today information, MissionAmerica.com, USPrayerTrack.com, Gospel.com, Church on the Web or one of the many new ones forming regularly. These sites will link you to a whole world of information, materials, opportunities and connections for further study.
- Zero in on a few ministries that interest you—perhaps one in inner-city ministry, one in the prayer movements and one in cross-cultural missions work. Contact them, ask to be placed on their mailing lists and suggest that you are available for volunteer work! A broad overview of these ministries is published annually in *The Great Commission Handbook* from Berry Publishing in Wheaton, Illinois (Phone: 800-727-8609).
- Visit other ethnic churches in your area and enjoy the signs of revival expressed in other cultural traditions.
- Listen on your local Christian radio station to the daily broadcast of the National Concert of Prayer and the five-minute breakthrough reports of Mission Network News. (If your station does not air these programs, put on your activist hat and talk with the station's program manager about carrying them!)
- Subscribe to key periodicals—or request your church or local public libraries to subscribe. Several great Christian periodicals are available that will sharpen your stand in the

Gap—such as *Christianity Today, World, New Man, Pray!* and *In Concert.* Subscribe to Evangelical Mission Information Service. Ask your pastor and church leaders for the key periodicals within your stream of Christendom, but don't leave your reading to one perspective; you may find yourself in a pea-sized box of Christianity! Consider regularly perusing secular publications such as:
— *National Geographic*
— *The World & I*
— *World Press*
— *The Economist*
— *International newspapers* (available in large public or university libraries) and the international sections of American megacity newspapers.
- Sit at the feet of missionaries, internationals and others from various people groups and countries who can tell you stories and breakthroughs of what God is doing among other peoples.

LINK WITH OTHER AGENTS OF REVIVAL

Intentionally plan to connect with others who also desire to be prisoners of hope. Set aside time to gather, discuss Scriptures about standing in the Gap, revival, faith and your role in God's plan. Exchange reports about how God is working toward revival right now. (One good resource is a 30-minute video with a discussion guide from the National Prayer Committee titled *Get Ready: Christian Leaders Speak Out on the Coming Revival.* See Resources.) Talk about how to be more spiritually prepared for what is coming. And most of all, pray together.

This pair, triplet, group or network will eventually be a solid team—a "revival team"—that serves as a base for fulfilling the vision by actively reaching out to the world in love. (See the following.)

Obviously, in order to gather with such a group to study and think through Gap issues, you will need to share your vision with others. This leads to the second ingredient in obeying the vision: Give it away!

GIVE THE VISION AWAY!

Key Questions: Am I multiplying my vision? Am I seeking out other Christians to stand in the Gap and hasten the coming revival?

External barriers are not the only ones hindering the fulfillment of another Great Awakening. Barriers within the Church may be just as critical. Along with cultural, linguistic and political barriers, we face internal barriers of provincialism and self-centeredness that afflict many. When any Christian's perspective and life direction revolves around pea-sized concerns, less will happen for Christ's cause than might have otherwise.

Christians must be alerted to the thousands of outreach opportunities awaiting their personal involvement right now, here and worldwide. Only then can we hope to close the Gap in our generation.

If you are part of a team, you can effectively awaken others who are sleeping through the greatest advance of all times and help the whole Body of Christ to support His cause. As you pass along discoveries from your own journey in discipleship, you can close the Gap of Unbelief and increase the total force involved in God's worldwide harvest. You and your growing team need to plan to share the vision.

This "revival team" as well as your church does not exist by accident, nor has God brought you together only for fellowship and survival. You can be certain that His Spirit intends for each believer to grow around one overriding cause: to stand in the Gap. Can you imagine the stirrings of revival you would see if *each* of your fellow believers suddenly began crying out that God would, as the Susan Ashton song "You Moved Me" puts it, "move me out of myself and into the fire."

You cannot hawk the vision or manipulate people, of course. You cannot force spiritual growth. If in your zeal to stand in the Gap, you begin pushing your fellow believers, they will push back. If you're so overzealous with vision that you "sunburn" people, they will avoid any more exposure to you! But you *can* encourage each person within your church to:

- Catch a big-picture vision of Christ and His global cause;
- Keep that vision at the center of their lives; and
- Obey that vision faithfully.

Your efforts to transfer your team's vision to other small groups might lead them to become yet another team standing in the Gap, working on the same basic plan for obeying the vision:

- Build the vision regularly.
- Give the vision to other believers.
- Fulfill the vision by reaching out directly in love.
- Pray the vision back to God.

Any attempt to give your vision to others involves your team in three major roles: You are a *model*—making the vision understandable and believable. You are a *catalyst*—making the vision inescapable and desirable. You are a *resource*—making the vision workable and manageable.

Give the vision as a model.
Make the vision of getting ready for revival, of standing in the Gap, understandable and believable. Set a quiet example before your group or church of what a person "standing in the Gap" really looks like. Without fanfare, carry through on your team's plan to obey your vision day by day. Slowly others will begin to realize that being this kind of messenger of hope clearly fits today's Christian and his or her concerns, that it produces significant results and that it fulfills all we are meant to be.

Think of your team as a model for what every Christian and every small group should desire to be. You are not a specialized "revivalist fringe" within your group or church. Avoid this fanatic image at all costs. Instead, help others recognize you as a vanguard, setting an exciting pace in Christian living that everyone would want to follow.

Give the vision as a catalyst.
Once you are providing a good model you will have the credibility to take a more direct role in motivating fellow Christians to get into the mainstream of the cause. As catalysts, you create an environment in which others can also catch a world vision as you make it inescapable and desirable for them.

In this second role your team resembles a time-release capsule. Slowly you release into the bloodstream of your group or church facts and challenges about what God is doing. Along with the information, you also seek to help provide practical ways to get a "feel" for what it means to reach out in the Gap. You invite one or two believers along with you when you distribute food to street kids, when you visit a

‡‡

The more a group becomes pro-activist, the more it needs "activist pros"!

‡‡

church of another ethnicity that is spiritually revived, when you take a short-term trip to Mongolia.

Give the vision as a resource.
The more a group becomes pro-activist, the more it needs "activist pros"! So in time, your team assumes a third role: resource. You make the Gap-standing experience workable and manageable for others.

A good resource needs to stay a few steps ahead of the pack. Your faithfulness to build your vision will naturally equip you to serve in this capacity. As a resource your team should help others see the ways God is already bringing signs of a river of revival, touching the ends of the earth. Then help them develop new directions and plans to impact others in the Gap. Train them to obey the vision through building it, giving it to others and reaching out.

You may be a resource for a number of people: the leadership of your group or church, new activists and "almost-activists," small groups who want more of a world-Christian dimension and people investigating prayer training, reconciliation information or cross-cultural opportunities.

Stand in the Gap has two companion volumes that can be tremendously helpful to you: *Messengers of Hope: Becoming Agents of Revival for the 21st Century* (Baker) spells out practical ways for sharing a vision for revival day after day; *The Hope at Hand: National and World Revival for the 21st Century* (Regal) defines many dimensions of the coming awakening, and lays out seven major confidence-builder reasons you can share with others so they too can prepare for and pray for revival without any fear of being disappointed. *The Hope at Hand* has a separate study guide, *Take It to Your Friends*, which you can use to guide a group through 12 weeks of discussing the vision. And of course, *Stand in the Gap* has a built-in study guide at the back of this book. Consider walking through this book with your Sunday School class for starters. All of these tools will equip you to serve as one who gives the vision away.

FULFILL THE VISION: REACH OUT IN LOVE

Key Question: Am I directly involved in the cause?

Dreamers! Awake! It's okay to dream about all the ways you might stand in the Gap, how your fellowship might get ready for a coming Great Awakening to Christ and how you will reach out in love. Prisoners of hope make the best kind of dreamers. Their growing vision drives them to dream of new ways to let their lives count for Christ's cause. Together they gather the big, world-sized dreams God gives to set them free in love to the ends of the earth!

If we build our vision on a regular basis, we will easily dream about effective personal ways to reach out. But dreaming is not enough. We must *act* on our visions. Without action we will eventually slumber off with heads full of interesting facts and unfulfilled dreams. Direct involvement is essential for the journey into cause-focused discipleship. Typical action steps to fulfill the vision often include these five areas:

- Reach out in prayer;
- Prepare for future outreach;
- Reach out in reconciliation;
- Reach out within my own people;
- Reach out into another people group.

Most active groups of world Christians will eventually move out on all five fronts, depending of course on where they are standing in the Gap. But getting active in all these areas will take time. Where should you begin?

Prayer is always the first action step. In fact, all the other reach-out options are reachable within the domain of prayer. We will focus on that crucial outreach effort in chapter 10. For now, let's consider your physical, in-person outreach plans.

Prepare for future outreach.
Getting ready for future outreach runs concurrent with the other five involvements. We agents of revival are always preparing to do more and do it more effectively. So this area should be in our plans from the beginning.

Reach out in reconciliation.
You may need to be personally reconciled with another believer. This is not the same as giving away your vision to others who will want to stand with you in the Gap. This is righting wrongs, asking forgiveness, repenting, restoring, confessing within the Church.

You will further want to explore actions that take you outside your church into the community to right wrongs, ask for forgiveness and so on. And consider crossing cultural and international barriers to implement reconciliation. Very clearly, the Spirit is telling us today that racial reconciliation within the Church is essential if we are to have a ministry of reconciliation with the gospel at wider ends of the Gap. Raleigh Washington's *Forgiveness and Reconciliation* will give you some background and ideas to step out in obedience to this ministry in the Gap. (See Resources.)

Reach out in your own people group.
Go ahead: Get radical and plan an activity that will tap into the "feeder streams" of revival that can come to your own church in your own culture. That is:

- Contact Concerts of Prayer International for materials to host your own churchwide or citywide Concert of Prayer. (See Resources.)
- Form a revival-focused prayer group to pray for spiritual breakthrough in the various areas of the Gap.
- Plan and implement a National Day of Prayer event.
- Do what you can to facilitate your youth group's partici-

pation in the See You at the Pole events and the Locker-2-Locker followups.

- Join hands with Evangelicals for Social Action to focus especially on the poor, the elderly, abortion and other "ethics of life" issues.
- Throw your lot in with the Family Research Council as it presses for political legislation to counter the flood of moral decay on many fronts.

Reaching out to those in your own fellowship is one thing. Much more intimidating is the prospect of action that steps out into the community and nation. If God has not already given you a sense of joy and eagerness about evangelism, about standing up for godly issues, about giving cups of cold water in Jesus' name, don't back down from this strategic area of reaching out.

Schedule yourself into a definite action step, an event to reach out beyond your church walls to those lost in the Gap. Many solid resources exist to stir your heart and train your skills to reach out in love to those around you who are, even though they live near dozens of churches, still without God and without hope.

In it all, be sure to keep up to speed with the coalition called Mission America, representing the whole spectrum of evangelical denominations and ministries. Mission America's goal is to bring the gospel to every American by the beginning of the twenty-first century—and to do so out of a heaven-sent national revival.

Reach out into another people group.

This action step in obeying the vision is not last on the list. Jesus told us to be His witness "both" or "simultaneously" in Jerusalem, Judea, Samaria and the uttermost parts of the earth. You may opt to *begin* your reaching out in this aspect of obedience. Because those at the widest end of the Gap are usually "out of sight" from us, they are usually "out of mind" as well. God has a heart for all peoples, particularly those who are the lonely, lost sheep of our world—the cultural groups we call the unreached peoples.

You can plan today to stand in the Gap for the unreached peoples of the world in several ways:

- Schedule your budget now to begin supporting a mission-ary and/or missions project.
- Discuss with your accountability partner and your develop-ing "revival team" the idea of sending out a mission team. Some will go and some will stay to be the sending support segment of the team. The "going" may only be across town, because many representatives of the world's least reached peoples live right here in North America. This is especially true for all of us living and serving in one of the 40 great urban centers of America such as Chicago or New York.
- Encourage your fellowship to join a mission service organi-zation—regardless of your denominational affiliation—to sharpen your skills for reaching out cross-culturally. One such association is ACMC—Advancing Churches in Mission Commitment. Another is AIMS—The Association of Inter-national Mission Services. (See Resources.)
- Help fund the missionary work of a Two-Thirds-World church organization or missionary society. Talk with your church missions departments or with Partners International. (See Resources for contacts.)
- Get involved in hunger-relief programs, especially those that combine Christ's saving love for the body and the soul. (See Resources for contacts.)
- With your team and/or your church, reach out to a refugee family in your city. (See Resources for contacts.)
- Support a homeless or destitute child in another part of the world through an evangelical child-sponsorship program. (See Resources for contacts.)
- Help support Christians living under oppression or depriva-tion, and thus strengthen their witness where they live. (See Resources for contacts.)
- Look for projects suggested in the periodicals of missions societies. Or write them asking for particular concerns or needs of the people groups that interest you.
- Discuss the possibility of supporting a project with a mis-sionary who visits with you. Find out how you can support some effort that mission team is making in evangelism right

now. Ask the same questions by letter to missionaries you know on the field.

- Give your support to groups or congressional representatives who actively promote human rights, especially where such support could affect the welfare of unreached people for whom you are praying or when pressure on dehumanizing regimes might stimulate a new degree of religious freedom in an unevangelized country. (See Resources for contacts.)
- Contribute to training centers, seminaries and centers for misssionary research to help prepare a future generation of missionaries and develop more effective missionary strategies. (See Resources for contacts.)
- Join the effort to place a Bible in their own language into the hands of each person listed in every phone directory in the world. (See Resources for contacts.)

There is a whole world out in the Gap. You can start your plans now to impact the widest part of the Gap through sacrificial, intimidating and yet significant outreach. Fulfill the vision of reaching out to the world—in love!

PLANNING YOUR OBEDIENCE

How can we put all this together in a specific plan to obey the vision? Glad you asked! Think through the following personal strategy outline.

A Personal Strategy Guide
For the next months my strategy will include three *main components:*

I Will Obey My Vision as I Regularly Build It

1. I will spend approximately _____ hours total each week in *a personal effort to build my vision of standing in the Gap.* That time will be divided into approximately _____ hours with one or more other believers who may become a sort of "revival team" and _____ hours working on my own.
2. How will I do it? When and where will I focus on this?

3. Topics: Of all I could study, I will begin with:

____ The Purpose: God's plan. A resource I'll start with is (See Resources for suggestions.):

____ The Possibilities: God's work in our world. A resource I'll start with is:

____ My Part: Where I fit. Resource I'll start with:

4. How will I know progress has happened? How will I measure it?
5. How will I know it is time to add something more?

I WILL OBEY MY VISION AS I GIVE IT TO OTHER CHRISTIANS

1. The time I spend each week giving my vision will be _____ hours.
2. I will begin by giving my vision to:
   Friends
   Family
   My small group
   My Bible study class
   My campus fellowship
   My church
   Others:
3. How will I do this? What do I see happening each week? What will be my resources and tools?
4. What will I do on my own? What will I do with a team?
5. How will I know when progress has happened? How will I measure it?
6. How will I know when it is time to add something more?

I WILL FULFILL MY VISION AS I REACH OUT DIRECTLY IN LOVE

1. The time I spend each week reaching out will be ____ hours.
2. The block of time I will spend this year in a dedicated outreach effort will be (dates):_____.

3. Of the five opportunities to reach out, I will begin with:
   - Reaching out in prayer;
   - Preparing for future outreach;
   - Reaching out in reconciliation;
   - Reaching out within my own people;
   - Reaching out into another people group.

4. How will I work on the areas I select? What do I see happening each week? What will be my resources and tools?
5. What will I do on my own? What will I do with a team?
6. How will I know when progress has happened? How will I measure it?
7. How will I know when it is time to add something more?

Still too vague? The following is a simple plan you might want to step into, make your own and eventually shape into your personal plan to obey the vision:

PERSONAL STRATEGY IN DAILY DISCIPLINE
THE 5-4-3-2-1 PLAN

Build Your Vision

5: Spend five minutes some time each day in personal devotions discovering something of what Scripture teaches about the great hope we have in serving Christ's global cause.

4: Spend an additional four minutes reading current revival-related and world-related literature such as a magazine article.

Give the Vision to Others

3: Sometime, each day, in personal conversation with another Christian (such as your family at evening meal or in a Bible study group, or in a letter), share for three minutes what God has given you in the previous nine minutes of building your vision.

Reach Out to the World in Love

2: Every day take two minutes to carry out a mission to the world. Of course, intercessory prayer allows you to do this, using what God gave you in the previous 12 minutes of building your vision. We will look at this more closely in the next chapter. Prayer is the simplest place to start. But you could also write a note to a missionary friend encouraging his or her ministry to unreached peoples. Or phone a nonChristian neighbor to chat a few minutes just to keep building that relationship.

1: That averages out to 14 minutes per day. Finally, before retiring at night, give God one more minute of complete quiet when He can speak to you about who you are becoming as a prisoner of hope, based on the other aspects of your daily disciplines as a disciple.

Fifteen minutes a day. Anyone can do it. Who among us cannot find or release an extra quarter-hour out of 24 hours to equip ourselves for the sake of Christ's cause and get ready for a coming national and world revival?

Of course, 15 minutes is just a beginning. Eventually you will become immersed in your God's-purpose-focused Bible study, or caught up in a discussion about the coming revival and its signs, or spend a whole meal with an international student from Indonesia. Before you know it, *hours* will fly by! But this basic 15 minutes will allow you to come to the close of each day saying with confidence:

> *I know this day my life has counted strategically toward a God-given awakening to Christ in my church, in my community and in my world.*

But we have not yet quite covered a basic, earth-shaking element of your standing in the Gap: Probably a bit more than you do now, you will need to *talk with God in the Gap.*

Note

1. Bill Bright and others, *Seven Promises of a Promise Keeper* (Colorado Springs: Focus on the Family Publishing, 1994), p. 8.

10 | GET READY: PRAY THE VISION!

STANDING IN THE GAP "BEFORE HIS FACE"
—WHERE EVERYONE BEGINS

⁘

I can still recall the moment. I was stunned. It came years after publication of the predecessor to this book (called at that time *In the Gap*). Sitting in my family room, during one of those rare quiet evenings at home alone, I happened to be grazing through my Bible just to feed my soul. Suddenly, right in the thick of scanning Ezekiel, I smacked into the text:

> I looked for a man among them who would build up the wall and stand before me in the gap on behalf of the land (Ezek. 22:30).

But my eyes focused on a phrase I'd never seen before: "...before me." Stand, yes, but do so *before God.* What did that mean?

I pulled down an Old Testament commentary to discover that the original Hebrew text reads: "before *My face.*" This was a phrase often used to describe the role of a priest in the temple. God saw them ministering before His face...in His presence...for His pleasure...at His call...to His glory.

Suddenly the whole plea of God in Ezekiel 22 took on a new dimension. Not only are we to build up the breach by putting ourselves into the thick of it, but we are also to do so as a people of prayer—a royal priesthood (see 1 Pet. 2:9). We are to represent God's heart *to* the nation (as messengers of hope) while, at the same time, interceding *for* the nation before God. That work of prayer is our ultimate hope that the Gap can be filled, the nation revived, the land spared, the enemies defeated and the purposes of God fulfilled throughout the earth.

That little "revelation" came to me in the spring of 1984. By June, I found myself helping to give leadership to the International Prayer

❖

THROUGH PRAYER WE CAN GO ANYWHERE IN THE GAP, TOUCH ANYONE, PRECIPITATE ANY MINISTRY AND REAP ANY IMPACT. PRAYER KNOWS NO BOUNDS.

❖

Assembly for World Evangelization. Sponsored by two worldwide networks of Christian mission and church leaders, it rallied nearly 3,000 prayer mobilizers from 70 nations to spend a week together. We were to pray for world revival and to strategize ways to get Christians everywhere praying as well.

I recall sitting on the platform on opening night, looking out over the sea of faces and marveling that in our day God could say, not "I found none" but rather, "I found thousands." Today, however, He can truly say, "I find *millions!*"

This is the place for you to begin your own stand in the Gap.

Stand there with the hundreds of men who recently joined in locations throughout the Northeast in a Men's All-Night Prayer Meeting. For seven hours throughout the night, they cried out to God with passion and determination for revival in our cities. Many of them came from New York City, where I live, and where a multi-ethnic, multi-denominational prayer movement has been unfolding for nearly a decade.

Here in one of the world's premiere "global cities," thousands of believers are coming before God's face on behalf of Christ's kingdom. Multitudes of them intercede in a round-the-clock prayer vigil called The Lord's Watch. Many of the pastors, who themselves have spent days together praying for New York, have entered into a covenant to which they are calling their congregations. This covenant expresses the vision

I'm finding in countless prisoners of hope who are standing in the Gap today. It reads:

> With repentance and hope, as leaders of Christ's Church in Metro New York City, we covenant to unite in prayer to seek God for revival in the Church, reconciliation among the churches, reformation in society and reaching the lost. We call others to join in praying with us until God answers, and then to take action as He does.

In other words: Build up the wall. Stand before God's face—in the Gap.

You Won't Be Lonely!

As we've seen, much needs to be done in Christ's global cause. But we can never do more than this: to grow as men and women of prayer and to mobilize others with us into a movement of prayer for spiritual awakening and world evangelization.

Through prayer we can go anywhere in the Gap, touch anyone, precipitate any ministry and reap any impact. Prayer knows no bounds. We are not just talking about private prayer, as essential as that is. We are also talking about *united* prayer—the most potent kind, and the kind that nearly 90 percent of the biblical teaching describes: "If two of you on earth agree about anything you ask for, it will be done for you by my Father in heaven.... Whatever you bind on earth will be bound in heaven, and whatever you loose on earth will be loosed in heaven" (Matt. 18:19,18).

For years I have called such efforts "concerts of prayer," a phrase used by prayer groups that sought God's face during the past three Great Awakenings.

As we worked through our *Stand in the Gap* study, were you struck by the recurring accounts of the millions involved in prayer events across our nation and the globe? As you take your stand in the Gap before His face, remember: *You are not alone!* Millions—literally—are standing there with you. This is *God's* prayer movement. Considering the magnitude of the numbers of prayers and their vision for revival, what must God be getting ready to do?

What better way for *us* to get ready for what He does than to stand in the Gap before Him in prayer?

Washington, D.C. is the place. Hundreds of thousands of men gathering for one purpose: A day of repentance and prayer. We come "on our knees in humility and on our feet in unity," says Promise Keepers founder Bill McCartney. We come confessing the sins of the nation...seeking heaven's throne for an outpouring of the Holy Spirit in national revival. What is the challenge to us? It's focused on the title of the event: "Stand in the Gap"—based on (You guessed it!) Ezekiel 22:30.

But the event also has a subtitle: "A Sacred Assembly of Men"—a concept taken from the book of Joel.

Your Prayers—Streaming to the River of Revival

Israel, in sackcloth, left behind every other activity, desperate in the face of a devastating locust plague, and came to the threshold of the Temple. There the people cried out a twofold prayer: "Spare your people, O Lord"; and "Do not make your inheritance an object of scorn, a byword among the nations. Why should they say among the peoples 'Where is their God?'" (Joel 2:17).

The men of Israel were praying for revival in the nation, and for God's testimony to prevail throughout the earth. And God's answer? He stated clearly: I will restore the years the locusts have eaten (see v. 25). I will pour out His Spirit upon all flesh (see v. 28). I will bring the nations into the valley of decision (see 3:14). I will return to dwell in Zion in all My fullness (see v. 21).

This is exactly what God was appealing for through Ezekiel. This is what it means to stand in the Gap together. And these are the wonders God is waiting to perform for those who will stay poised before His face.

Is any mission greater? Of course, we need to catch, keep and obey the vision. But before it all, under it all, out ahead of it all, we must first *pray* the vision. Our prayers prepare us and also prepare the way for the coming revival as nothing else can. Even more, our prayers actually become the fountainhead for the very revival we seek. The "feeder streams" bring forth the "river of revival."

None of this should surprise us, however. For *the* Man who stands in the Gap, the One who stands before the Father's throne on behalf of all peoples, has never ceased to intercede (see Heb. 7:24,25) since the day all authority was given Him in heaven and on earth (see Matt. 28:18). His intercession is the very basis of what He is doing—extending His scepter among the nations and ruling in the midst of His enemies (see Ps. 110:1-3,4). Why should we think that it would be any different for us who follow Him—for us who are united with Him?

So *stand!*

- Get strategically positioned.
- Be counted with those who are making a difference.
- Be aggressive and persistent. No "slouching" allowed!
- Stay alert. Keep watching. Be ready to move as the answers come. Remain "on call."

Do so *before God's face.*

- God is the only hope for our nation and our generation. Look nowhere else.
- Seek the revelation of His very person until His "countenance shines upon us."
- Worship Him face-to-face, seeing Him for who He really is.
- Serve Him in your priestly role. Lift up holy hands on behalf of the land. And stay before His face!

ALL YOU HAVE TO DO IS BEGIN

Does this sound like too much to bear? Do you feel inadequate for such a ministry of prayer? Are you afraid you will fail such a calling? Well, I have good news for you. Not only is God searching for such people to stand in the Gap, but He is the One who will fulfill this work in and through them.

Just as revival is a sovereign work of God, even so all the prayers preceding the coming revival spring from the heart of God. They are given to us to pray by the Holy Spirit who prays within us (see Rom. 8:26,27). Paul points out that the Spirit's prayers within us tie in with God's plan for the whole earth.

Isaiah understood this. In Isaiah 59:1,2 the Gap of Sin—our "separation"—is described. Subsequent verses (see especially vv. 12-14) tell us how very serious sin is. Above all, God says He is amazed that He cannot find one person to stand in that Gap to intercede (see vv. 15,16). He rolls up His sleeves and steps into the Gap Himself (see vv. 15,16) with uncompromising zeal for His saving purposes (see v. 19). In fact, ultimately the Redeemer Himself appears in the Gap (see v. 20).

But then, Isaiah tells us, God turns around and puts the same words and the same Spirit into *all* of His people, so that they start doing what He's doing because He does it in and through them (see v. 21)! The result? Well, listen:

> "Arise, shine, for your light has come, and the glory of the Lord rises upon you" (60:1). That's revival.

> Next: "Nations will come to your light, and kings to the brightness of your dawn" (60:3). That's world evangelization.

The Gap has been transformed! Why? Because first God Himself stood in the Gap. And then He mobilized countless others to do the same...through prayer.

Is God mobilizing you to stand in the Gap? If so, how do you begin to stand before His face? Where do you start? Fortunately, a myriad of books on prayer have hit the bookstores these days—most are helpful on the why, how and what of prayer. Maybe you would like to begin with my little volume *Concerts of Prayer: Christians United for Spiritual Awakening and World Evangelization.*

But the crucial thing is that you *begin!* Get away with God for 15 minutes a day, or even start with five minutes. Take *Stand in the Gap* for a reference; use its vision as your initial agenda. Start to talk with God about the issues we have explored in this book—issues that touch your life, your church, your community, your nation and even unreached peoples of the world. Let your heart be broken before His face for all the concerns of Christ's global cause.

Then, covenant with two or three others to meet with you at church for just 10 minutes once a week. Perhaps meet between Sunday School and morning worship, find a corner of the building, put your heads together and begin to pray—in the Gap, for the Gap, to fill the Gap. Simple? Sure. Easy? No—because during that 10 minutes, you are still, truly, taking a stand. You are before God's face. And miracles will happen.

The challenge is: Begin. Now. Take the time. Make the time. Can you find the time? If not for this, then for what? What else really matters until we begin to "pray the vision," standing in the Gap.

Not long ago, the coach of Northwestern University basketball called for all Christians in the United States to set aside the first week of February, to turn off their TVs, and use that time period each day to fast, pray and refocus their attention on what the cause of Christ is really all about. He called it simply, "Time Out!"

So let me ask you: Do you want to be ready for the coming revival? Do you want to be a part? Then let me conclude this book with one small suggestion: Call, "Time out!" Because it is time...time to stand in the Gap.

Stand in the Gap:
The Small-Group Bible Study

⁙

Your Guide for a 12-Session
Study of This Book

⁙

Discussion Leader's Guide

Although this book has 10 chapters, the study fits easily into any length of series from 5 to 12 sessions:

Five Sessions
If you have 5 sessions, discuss two chapters per session, choosing from the following 10-session outline the learning activities you will use. Be sensitive to the needs and interests of your group to know which chapters should be given the most attention and which ones require less time in your discussions.

Ten Sessions
If you have 10 sessions, discuss one chapter per session.

Twelve Sessions
If you have 12 sessions, discuss one chapter per session, plus the following two additional sessions:

- Introductory Session: Follow instructions 1-7. Either in small groups (up to six), or with the entire group together, lead participants in one of the following options:

A. View the video *Get Ready: Christian Leaders Speak Out on the Coming Revival* (available by phoning 630-690-8441). Simply discuss the comments made on the video. Introduce the *Stand in the Gap* course. (See instruction #1 following.) Close in group prayer for personal, churchwide, nationwide and worldwide revival.

B. In place of the video (mentioned in introductory session A), take turns reading and commenting on any number of the breakthroughs listed in *Stand in the Gap*:

> Chapter 1
> Chapter 2
> Chapter 7

If every participant will not have a book for this first session, consider permission as granted for you to photocopy these lists of breakthroughs. Cut the lists into slips of paper with one item each and distribute throughout the group.

Next, introduce the overall course and close in group prayer for personal, churchwide, nationwide and worldwide revival.

- For a twelfth session, consider the following options:

A. In a closing review session, guide participants to overview the main points of each chapter. An especially interesting review at this point might be discussion about the Introduction: "From One Egg to Another." Simply scan each chapter's subtitled sections and call for comments or questions. Then discuss implementing some of the concepts from *Stand in the Gap*:
  - What are two steps each of us will take to personally prepare for the coming revival?
  - What is one thing we can do as a group to stand in the Gap?
  - What is one practical action step and one key prayer

point we as a church can implement to get ready for a
coming national revival?

- If we set another time to gather, who will bring information about an unreached culture at the widest end of
the Gap so we can pray and strategize on how that people can be reached with the good news of Jesus Christ?

The optimum-sized discussion group is 10 to 15 individuals. With a
smaller group, interest may taper off unless there is a high level of commitment on everyone's part. A larger group will require strong leadership skills to help everyone participate meaningfully.

1. Read *Stand in the Gap* yourself. Mark key points that might
   especially apply to your study group.
2. If you are leading a group that already meets regularly, such
   as a Sunday School class or Bible study group, decide how
   many weeks to spend on the series and set your dates.

   Consider holidays or other events that might affect the
   continuity of attendance. In most cases 5 to 10 sessions is a
   good length of time to adequately deal with the major
   issues in the book.
3. Beginning at the first session, arrange seating informally,
   either in one semicircle or several smaller circles of no
   more than eight chairs per circle.
4. Provide each person with a copy of the book and a typed
   schedule for the series. In most cases, people will put more
   into the series—both at home and at the sessions—if they
   buy the book themselves.
5. Briefly share one or two ways in which this book has ben-
   efited you, the leader. This sharing should not be a sales
   pitch for the book.

   The group will appreciate your being a fellow learner.
   Sharing insights gained from this book is a good approach
   to beginning any session of the series. As the series pro-
   gresses, prompt one or two participants to open each session as you did in this first session—by sharing one or two
   thoughts from the book that sparked ideas.

6. In each session, lead group members in following instructions and discussing the questions from each chapter as listed below.

   The discussion topics are arranged to first **define** or focus on the issues in the chapter. Then participants are asked to dig into the Word to **discover** more of what God says on the topic. Next the discussion questions guide the group to **decide** how to apply a concept. And finally the session closes with an action plan—what we can **do** as a result of the lesson.

   If you have more than 8 or 10 participants in your group, assign some of the questions to be discussed in smaller groups, then invite each group to share one or two insights with the larger group. Alternate large-group and small-group discussions to provide variety and to allow every group member to comfortably participate.

7. In guiding the discussions, the following tips are helpful:
   - If a question or comment is raised that is off the subject, suggest it either be dealt with at another time or ask the group if they would prefer to pursue the new issue now.
   - If someone talks too much, direct a few questions specifically to other people, making sure not to put a shy person in the spot. Talk privately with the "dominator," asking for his or her cooperation to help draw out a few of the quieter group members.
   - If someone does not participate verbally, assign a few questions to be discussed in pairs, trios or other small groups. Or distribute paper and pencils and ask people to write their answers to a specific question or two. Then invite several people, including the "shy" one, to read what they wrote.
   - If someone asks a question and you do not know the answer, admit it and move on. If the question calls for insight about personal experience, invite group members to comment.
   - If the question requires specialized knowledge, offer to

look for an answer in the library, from your pastor or from some other appropriate resource before the next session.

8. Pray regularly for the sessions and the participants.

STUDY SESSIONS

For a 12-lesson course, see the previous suggestions for an opening introductory session and a twelfth closing session. For a 5-lesson course, combine pairs of sessions. Otherwise, for a 10-lesson course, use the following outline:

Session One—Chapter 1

::

There Is a Gap...and You're in It Right Now!
Facing the Gap—From Toledo to Timbuktu

Define: Ezekiel was an Old Testament prophet who warned Israel of impending judgment before he and most of the population were taken captive to Babylon nearly 600 years before Christ. His name means "God strengthens."

- What is your sense today of "impending judgment"?
- Why is the message that "God strengthens" important today?

Discover: Take turns reading verses to catch the context of standing in the Gap: Read Ezekiel 22:23-29.

- What were the characteristics of God's people at that time?
- What is the significance of the fact that judgment would come not because of the conduct of unbelievers but of God's people?
- What are the various "stages" of the Gap that God desires to close? (Guide your discussion using the diagram of The Gap in this chapter.)
- What would happen if no one stood in the Gap? Discuss Bryant's three suggestions under the subtitle "What Is This Gap?"

Decide: The antidote to the despair of impending judgment is hope. Read together Paul's prayer for us in Ephesians 1:18-23. We can be people of hope in the midst of doom and gloom because our God has called us to hope. Will we respond? Take turns reading the evidences of our hope as listed in chapter 1.

Do: Spend a few minutes in silent prayer. Consider asking God for confidence to be one He can count on to stand in the Gap.

- Commit to share with at least one person a few of the evidences for hope you've discussed.
- If you haven't yet read *Stand in the Gap* chapter 1, read it carefully as a review of this session.
- Read *Stand in the Gap* chapter 2 in preparation for the next session.

Session Two—Chapter 2

::

Coming to the Gap: A Great Awakening to Christ
*The Confident Hope That Can Revolutionize
Your Life Forever*

Define: On scratch paper, doodle a timeline of what might be the rest of your life. (Be as tongue-in-cheek or serious as you choose!) Now add somewhere along that possible timeline, the occurrence of an explosive spiritual awakening. Discuss:

- How might a stunning national and worldwide revival affect your personal life?
- How might you be involved?

Discover: Have someone read or take turns reading Ezekiel 47:1-12. This remarkable passage obviously calls for further in-depth study. For now, however, discuss the following:

- The best commentary on Scripture, of course, is Scripture. What do the following passages add to our understanding of Ezekiel's vision? (Assign each passage to pairs or small groups to think through and report on their insights.)

John 4:7-14   Titus 3:4-6
John 7:37-39   Revelation 21:6

- If Ezekiel is describing his encounter with a fresh outpouring of the Holy Spirit, how do you suppose he *feels?* In control? Confused? Cleansed?
- Read through Orr's and Packer's descriptions of revival in this chapter. How do these characteristics compare to the particulars of Ezekiel's vision?

Decide: Look together at the "River of Revival" diagram. How many specific examples can you list of these "feeder streams" of revival? Which of these, if any, are you involved in as a group?

Do: Discuss:

- What is one thing each member of the group can do this week to participate in "feeding" this river of revival? Perhaps contract to phone each other midweek to encourage accountability in this action step.
- Close in prayer, asking God for revival to come to us personally, as a fellowship, as a nation and for a worldwide spiritual awakening to Jesus Christ.
- Read and jot notes through chapter 3 in preparation for your next session.

Session Three—Chapter 3

⁚⁚

Retreating from the Gap: The Curse of Pea-Sized Christianity
Boxes That Blind Us to the Hope Before Us

Define: Discuss how each of you might answer a couple of Bryant's questions about "The Greatest of All Gaps":

1. "Why, with more than a third of a million churches in America, hasn't true, good-news Christianity penetrated the fields of science, politics and the media—much less penetrated the homes of our neighborhoods?"
2. "Why, after 2,000 years of countless possibilities for world evangelization by an international Church, are more than 2 billion people still unevangelized, most of whom have not even heard Christ's name?"

Discover: Divide into pairs or small groups, discuss and then report on:

- The significance of the following passages about the greatest of all Gaps:

Matthew 13:54-58
Luke 19:37-44

- The clarity of the task set before God's people:

Genesis 12:1-3
2 Corinthians 5:18-20

Decide: How do you react to the boxes of "pea-sized Christianity" and the reasons for them?

- Take turns reading the list of "boxes" and have the rest of the group call out reactions/comments to each one.
- Discuss one, two or all three of the reasons Bryant gives for these boxes of pea-sized Christianity: *Narcissism, Smörgasborditis* and *Blindness.*
- Discuss the myths behind much of Christendom's apathetic attitude toward standing in the Gap.

Do: Bolster each others' desire to break out of boxes of pea-sized Christianity that blind us to the hope before us.

- Choose random items or read to each other the entire list

of what God is doing to prepare for a coming revival.
- Ask prayer of each other for any boxes, reasons or myths that seemed to describe our own unbelief.
- Remind each other to read chapter 4 in preparation for the next lesson.

Session Four—Chapter 4

::

Thriving in the Gap: What It Means to Be a "Prisoner of Hope"
Getting Serious About Revival

Define: Begin your session by simply discussing your ideas of what it means to be "a prisoner of hope."

Discover: Read through Zechariah 9:9-12. This passage specifically applies to Israel. Yet we can glean key lessons for our own lives as we discuss:

- Why would anyone rejoice and shout in triumph (v. 9) when threatened (v. 1)?
- Is it unrealistic to look toward peace and the complete dominion of Christ (v. 10)? Why or why not?
- What might a "waterless pit" be, and who are these "prisoners" (v. 11)?
- What are your insights about these "prisoners of hope" or "prisoners who have the hope" (v. 12)?
- What does it mean to "return to your fortress" (v. 12)? (See Jer. 16:19; Joel 3:16.)

Decide: This command to "return" suggests "repentance." Enjoy a prayer time together:

- Have someone read slowly through Bryant's list of areas of repentance, pausing after each entry to allow individuals to silently confess anything the Holy Spirit might suggest.
- Have the reader close in a prayer of praise that, as we

"return" in repentance, God transforms us into "prisoners of hope"!

Do: Choose one of the following options as an action step for this session. After the activity, as appropriate, close in prayer and remind each other to read chapter 5 for the next session. Choose one:

- Read the final paragraph before Bryant's "Tour of the Gap in Los Angeles" and individually list at least three specific answers to "What would your life look like if you became bound up in hope?"
- Split up as a group, with each individual finding a quiet place to spend more time in personal prayers of repentance.
- Quickly brainstorm the various evidences of the Gap Bryant sees in his imaginary "Tour of the Gap in Los Angeles." Schedule a time when you'll join together in teams to actually tour your own community or a nearby city to similarly investigate evidences of the Gap.

Session Five—Chapter 5

::

Stand in the Gap: The Call to Get Ready
Your Jump Start into a Daily Discipleship Wrapped Around God's Plan for the Nations

Define: Begin your session by asking if anyone can finish the verse, "Be still, and...." With a few responses, look up together Psalm 46:10 and read aloud the remainder of the verse. What does this exercise suggest about focusing on *myself,* memorizing only promises about *myself,* thinking the Bible is a story about *me?*

Next, discuss group responses to a quote in chapter 5: "We don't save our lives by trying to save our lives; we experience the fullness of salvation as we give.... The larger the giveaway, the greater the growth."

Discover: As a group, look up and jot notes as you read through the following passages. Don't plan to study each passage in-depth. Simply use your notes for your "Decide" discussion.

Psalm 23:3   Ephesians 2:11-22
Psalm 67:1,2,7 Hebrews 10:23-25
Acts 1:8   1 John 5:14,15
Ephesians 2:10

Decide: Discuss what these passages and chapter 5 of *Stand in the Gap* suggest about broadening the scope of your personal discipleship. How does focusing *outward* rather than just inward affect:

- Your sense of the cause of Christ;
- Your understanding of God's blessing on your life;
- Your prayer life;
- Your Bible study;
- Your purpose in life;
- Your motives for godliness as He leads you in paths of righteousness;
- Your gathering with other believers in local fellowships;
- Your pursuit of reconciliation;
- Your reaching out in Jesus' name.

Do: Doodle a "diagram" of the various "compartments" of your life. Link the parts of the diagram with arrows or lines. As oddly difficult as this is, diagram what your life might look like if it were thoroughly integrated around the cause of Christ. If you choose, share your diagrams in pairs.

Close by praying for each other's desire to, as Elton Trueblood put it at the end of this chapter, unite all your powers, intellectual and emotional "into a single pattern of self-giving."

Session Six—Chapter 6

::

So, Who Will Stand in the Gap?
*You Were Brought to the Kingdom for Such
a Time as This*

Define: Give a pop quiz to each other as to your understanding of the following terms:

- Prisoner of hope
- Messenger of hope
- Agent of revival
- World Christian

Discover: Pair up and choose one of the following sets of questions. After about four to five minutes, share your insights with the entire group.

Set 1. Describe the results if no one were to stand in the Gap:
- Ezekiel 21:3,4
- Ezekiel 22:23-30

Set 2. Describe some of the results if God's people stood in the Gap:
- Psalm 33:12-22

Set 3. Read the following passages and pinpoint phrases in the verses that highlight the disciples' faith in Jesus' Person, His purpose and His promise:
- Luke 24:36-53
- Acts 1:1-8

Decide: Ask someone to read 1 John 1:1. For each item below, list at least two ways each of us can stand in the Gap to present a message of hope that is:

- Heard
- Seen (available)
- Looked upon (visible as a model)
- Touched

Do: Bryant asks two questions at the end of this chapter:

1. Will I stand in the Gap?
2. In what part of the Gap will I stand?

Spend a few minutes in silent prayer considering our responses to this challenge.

Remind each other to read chapter 7 for next session.

Session Seven—Chapter Seven

::

Get Ready: Catch the Vision!
A World Full of Purpose and Possibilities

Define: Take a silent poll about the following question. Participants jot their "yes" or "no" answer on a slip of paper, hand it in to one person who tallies the results. Then discuss briefly your findings.

- Do I actually believe we are going to experience a sweeping revival?

Discover: Discuss the following:

- Colossians 1:18-20. In what ways is Christ the center of God's purpose?
- Revelation 5:9. What does Bryant mean that the nations are the target of God's purpose?
- Romans 1:16,17; Isaiah 61:1,4,11. How can we rely on the gospel as the power of God's purpose?
- 1 Thessalonians 1:6-8. How can we be like the Thessalonian believers as the strategy of God's purpose?
- Colossians 1:3-7. In what ways is cultural transformation the impact of God's purpose?
- Revelation 12:9,11. What do these verses suggest about Satan, the enemy of God's purpose?
- From our studies so far, how would a sweeping national and worldwide revival be the acceleration of God's purpose in our day?

Decide: Divide into three smaller groups. Each will take one section of Bryant's discussion about a world full of possibilities and report key factors:

- Group 1: The Church's potential
- Group 2: The indications from Church history
- Group 3: The signals from today's prayer movements

Have someone conclude this section by reading and asking for comments about historian Richard Lovelace's quote at the end of chapter 7.

Do: First read Acts 4:29-31. Then review your "Define" polling results. As a whole group, pray about your individual responses to the questions:

- Do I actually believe we are going to experience a sweeping revival?
- If so, am I willing to share that hope with others—even if it might bring persecution?

Remind each other to read chapter 8 for next session.

Session Eight—Chapter 8

::

Get Ready: Keep the Vision!
Standing in the Gap with Heart, with Others, with a Plan

Define: As an opening, read Bryant's parable and ask for any observations or insights. Wrap up this "Define" section with a question: "Can we escape the sorcery of Christian self-centeredness?" Pray for the group.

Discover: Read and discuss as a group:

- Mark 8:34. What does it mean to follow Christ?
- Matthew 16:25. What does it mean to find my life?
- Acts 1:8 and 1 Corinthians 2:1-5. Why do we need the Holy Spirit? (Another way of asking the question is: What are we doing now that requires the Holy Spirit?)
- Ephesians 4:1-6. Who would be on a list of those within the Body of Christ with whom we need to be reconciled—as individuals, as a local church, as part of a denomination or affiliation of churches, as part of Christendom, as a culture, as a country?

Decide: Together scan the review of what we've studied so far.

Do: Pray, remind each other to study chapter 9 for next session, and break up to ponder and sign the *Standing in the Gap* commitment.

Session Nine—Chapter 9

∷

Get Ready: Obey the Vision!
Standing in the Gap As You Work Your Plan

Define: Read Bryant's comment: "God usually does not lead us on the basis of facts we do not have." Then suggest that the group brainstorm in pairs to schedule a personal time weekly when each will build her or his vision.

Discover: Read and discuss the following familiar passages in light of our study so far.

- Mark 12:30,31
- Matthew 28:19,20

Decide: Roll up your sleeves in preparation for a very practical period of applying some of the chapter 9 suggestions for obeying the vision. Take turns reading through the bulleted points of the following sections. Encourage each other to take notes about the action steps that seem personally important.

- Build the Vision
- Become Accountable
- Study
- Link Up with Other Agents of Revival

Next, discuss how you can:

- Give the vision to other believers as a model;
- Give the vision to other believers as a catalyst;
- Give the vision to other believers as a resource.

Then take turns reading through the bulleted suggestions on how to reach out in love. Encourage each other to jot notes on action steps that seem personally important.

- Reach Out in Your Own People Group
- Reach Out into Another People Group

Do: Work together in pairs to help each other begin filling in A Personal Strategy Guide. Use some of the suggestions noted during your "Decide" activity. The strategy plan is personal, so after a brief start in the session period, each participant must continue developing her or his plan later on his or her own time.

Wrap up the session with prayers for wisdom, and remind each other to read through chapter 10 for next session.

Session Ten—Chapter 10

::

Get Ready: Pray the Vision!
Standing in the Gap "Before His Face"
—Where Everyone Begins

Define: In this session on prayer "before His face," begin by moving through several steps of prayer. Each time the question to pray is: "What do You want us to do to stand in the Gap?"

- Open with a person leading the group in prayer.
- Pray silently as individuals.
- Pray conversationally, with participants praying in phrases or brief sentences as they feel led.
- Pray aloud all at once. This Asian prayer practice will encourage many who are reluctant to pray aloud in a group to blend their voices in with everyone's.
- Wait in silence as a group, practicing listening to God.
- The person who opened the prayer time closes in prayer.

Discover: Read and discuss:

- Ezekiel 22:30

- Joel 2:17,25,28; 3:14,21
- Matthew 18:18,19

Decide: Brainstorm one way in which a person might act on the following steps:
- Get strategically positioned to stand in the Gap.
- Be counted with those who are making a difference.
- Be aggressive and persistent.
- Stay alert and keep watching.
- Do all these steps "before His face."

Do: Begin now to stand in the Gap before His face. Spend more time in prayer for:

- Your personal revival;
- Your immediate family members and relatives;
- Your fellow believers and your local church;
- Non-Christians in your culture, your people group;
- Your country;
- Believers in other cultures and countries;
- Non-Christians in other cultures and countries.

After your prayer session, decide what comes next. See Resources for tools you can use to get ready for the coming revival, standing in the Gap.

- Start with prayer. A good study resource is Bryant's *Concerts of Prayer*. (See Resources.)
- Spend 15 minutes daily with God to discuss the issues covered. Perhaps use *Stand in the Gap* as a framework.
- Form small accountability groups to keep each other spiritually strong, to pray together and to work through resources to build your vision. Meet with each other for just 10 minutes per week—perhaps between your Bible study classes and church service.
- If you feel that your life plans have been particularly rattled by the study together, ask friends to pray that you will be

obedient to God's leading. You may find yourself standing in the Gap in Toledo! Or Timbuktu!

(For a 12-session study, see previously mentioned options.)

Sources and Resources

Tools to Get Ready for the Coming Revival

⚌

We could list literally hundreds of other key resources—because we're talking about the historic, eternal, global cause of Christ! But the following are some crucial materials for your *Stand-in-the-Gap* toolbox. Each will in turn point you to more key resources. Unless otherwise noted, the resource is available through your local Christian bookstore.

Salvation
Book: *More Than a Carpenter* by Josh McDowell (Living Books/Tyndale, 1977). For someone just beginning to explore Who God is and what He is doing, this classic on finding new life in Christ is a must read!

Revival
Book: *Revival Fire* by Wesley Duewel (Zondervan, 1995). Duewel guides the reader through centuries of revival highlights to give context to today's expectations of the coming national and world revival.

Book: *The Coming World Revival* by Robert Coleman (Crossway Books, 1995). Crafted by the Christian statesman who gave us *The Master Plan of Evangelism*, this book heightens our confidence in the pattern of what God has done and is doing to bring revival in our generation.

Prayer Training
Organization: Every Home for Christ offers the *Change the World School of Prayer* course which you and your small group can take by correspondence. Every Home for Christ is also a contact for outreach projects because it distributes Scripture portions throughout the world. Contact EHFC, P.O. Box 35930, Colorado Springs, CO 80935-3593, phone (719) 260-8888.

Building Vision
Study Course: *Perspectives on the World Christian Movement* is a demanding study of the biblical, historical, cultural and strategic aspects of what God is doing in the big picture. Contact the Perspectives Study Office for details: 1605

E. Elizabeth St., Pasadena, CA 91104, phone (818) 398-2125. A do-it-yourself local-church version of *Perspectives* is *Vision for the Nations* (Call 800-MIS-SION for information).

Giving Away Vision
Seminar Package: *Make A Difference: How to Mobilize Your Church to New Mission Vision* by ProclaMedia/World Christian, 1996. This audiotape, videotape and reproducible manual trains zealots to carefully and successfully share vision with the nonmission-minded of the fellowship. Available through ProclaMedia, 5050 Edison Dr., Colorado Springs, CO 80909, phone (719) 634-5310.

Reaching Out in Reconciliation
Book: *Forgiveness and Reconciliation* by Raleigh Washington (Destiny Images, 1996), heading Promise Keepers' reconciliation efforts, tells a tremendous story and also provides a practical manual on how you and your fellowship can stand in the Gap to resolve racial tensions in our society.

Reaching Out in Evangelism
Book: *How to Give Away Your Faith* by Paul Little (InterVarsity Press, 1977). This is a proven classic about how to share your faith in Jesus Christ with others in your own culture in the Gap.

Reaching Out Across Cultures
Activism: Become a host family for an international student. Contact International Students Inc., 2864 S. Circle Dr., Colorado Springs, CO 80906, phone (719) 576-2700.

Book: *Run With the Vision* by Bob Sjögren, Bill and Amy Stearns (Bethany House, 1995). "How to Mobilize, How to Send, How to Go" is the subtitle of this broad overview of God's global plan and how you can find your part in it— whether on the homefront or in another culture.

Planning for Outreach
Book and workbook: *Vacations with a Purpose* by Chris Eaton and Kim Hurst (David C. Cooke, 1993). Focused on the practical preparations for teams going on short-term ministry trips, this guidebook set is essential for launching intelligent outreach projects.

Information Sources
Electronic Information Source: *Brigada* is a cost-free network that will fill you in on basics and then direct you to other incredible information sources. Subscribe (or ask a friend with a computer and modem to subscribe for you) by sending to hub@xc.org the following message (with a blank space in the "subject" area): subscribe Brigada

A Guidance System: The LOOP is a cost-free guidance system for those wanting to send or be one of the new missionaries of the twenty-first century. It provides awareness, urges accountability and outlines preparations to step into the mission efforts of the individual's own church. Get into The LOOP by calling (800) 388-9915 in the United States.

An Association: Membership in World Christian—an association of "global activists for the cause of Christ"—brings a monthly interactive newsletter on revival, prayer, evangelism and missions. In-depth reports are accessible through fax-on-demand, e-mail, the WorldWide Web or by phone or mail. Members keep up-to-speed through weekly breakthrough updates, conferences and expeditions. Contact World Christian, e-mail 73502,3126@CompuServe.com, by mail at Box 1010, Colorado Springs, CO 80901, phone (719) 634-5310, fax (719) 634-5316.

Involvement

Contact the following organizations for events and opportunities for involvement:

Celebrate Jesus 2000 Events

Join with other believers to strategize how every person in America can be presented the Gospel by the end of the century. Contact Mission America, 901 East 78th St., Minneapolis, MN 55420, phone (612) 853-1762; fax (612) 853-1745; e-mail 74152,636@CompuServe.com

Fasting and Prayer Convocations

These annual events focus on humbling ourselves before God to usher in the coming revival. Contact Campus Crusade for Christ headquarters for information: 100 Sunport Lane, Dept. 2100, Orlando, FL 32809, toll-free phone (888) 327-8464; fax (888) 327-8772; e-mail fasting&prayer@cci.org and Website www.mdlink.com/ccc

National Day of Prayer

You can join and even help organize local events to acknowlege this annual celebration of prayer in behalf of our country. Contact the National Day of Prayer Committee, c/o Focus on the Family, P.O. Box 15616, Colorado Springs, CO 80935, phone (719) 531-3379.

National Network of Youth Ministries

You can participate in National Youth Forums, "See You at the Pole" events and other opportunities for youthworkers and youth. Contact the National Network of Youth Ministries, 12335 World Trade Drive, Suite 16, San Diego, CA 92128, phone (619) 451-1111.

Promise Keepers

From local accountability groups to national rallies, men can join in with hundreds of thousands of other Christian men to stand in the Gap. Contact Promise Keepers, P.O. Box 103001, Denver CO 80250-3001, phone (303) 964-7600.

Aglow International

Women of varying denominational backgrounds meet locally and in national conferences to encourage and equip each other for prayer, study and outreach. Contact Aglow International, P.O. Box 1749, Edmonds, WA 98020-1749, phone (206) 775-7282.

YOU'LL FIND IT HERE!

I f you're looking for outstanding prayer resources, look no further! Write or call today to request *COPI's* free product brochure, *Engaging God Together: Distinctive Resources for Mobilizing God's People to Pray.*

Detailed are more than 20 books, tapes, and videos along with descriptions, prices, and easy ordering instructions.

Simply mark the box below and return by mail or call *COPI's* 24-Hour Request Line at 1-800-576-6458.

Resources Order Form

Resource	Price	Quantity	Total
Together in Hope Manual and Two Videos	$49.99		
The Hope at Hand Book by David Bryant	$12.99		
Take It to Your Friends! Hope at Hand Study Guide	$ 4.99		
Messengers of Hope Book by David Bryant	$12.99		
Concerts of Prayer Book by David Bryant	$10.99		
Get Ready! Video with Discussion Guide	$14.99		
Engaging God Together Prayer Resource Brochure	FREE		
	SUBTOTAL *(this side):*		

Order Form continued on next page

DAVID BRYANT AND
CONCERTS OF PRAYER INTERNATIONAL

D avid Bryant is the founder and president of *Concerts of Prayer International (COPI)*, a multifaceted ministry that calls for, equips, and mobilizes "agents of revival" who seek God for spiritual awakening and worldwide evangelization.

COPI is committed to:

1. *Preaching and promoting a comprehensive vision of Jesus Christ and helping the Church remain clear on the awakening for which we are praying and preparing.*

2. *Equipping "agents of revival" as we network, train, and partner with those raised up by God into leadership for revival.*

3. *Strengthening the united prayer movement, expanding it, and keeping it focused and centered on Jesus Christ.*

The *COPI Team* welcomes the opportunity to be of assistance to you.

Resources Order Form

	Total
1. *Subtotal from other side*	
2. *Illinois Residents add 6.75% Sales Tax*	
3. *Shipping & Handling*	
a. $3.00 minimum	*$3.00*
b. If purchases total more than $20, add an additional 10% of Line 1.	
c. If shipping to Canada, add another 5% of line 1.	
d. If shipping overseas, add another 20% of Line 1.	
GRAND TOTAL ENCLOSED:	

Make your check payable to *Concerts of Prayer International (COPI)*.
Return by mail to: COPI • P.O. Box 1399 • Wheaton, IL 60189
Phone: 630-690-8441 • FAX: 630-690-0160

UPS will not deliver to a Post Office Box. Please provide street address for shipping:

Name _____

Address _____

City _____ State _____ Zip _____

Concerts *of* prayer

INTERNATIONAL
*for spiritual awakening &
worldwide evangelization*

TOGETHER IN HOPE:

How to Conduct a Concert of Prayer Rally in Your City or Church

Complete Package—Manual and Two Videotapes
An Outstanding Value at *$49.99*

A complete, step-by-step package for anyone who wants to learn how to organize a local Concert of Prayer rally. This material was developed from years of leading Concerts of Prayer in over 350 cities nationwide. You'll receive a five-part training manual, an hour-long informational training video featuring David Bryant and Steve Bell from *Concerts of Prayer International,* and an additional video showing an actual Concert of Prayer event led by David Bryant.

In addition to detailed guidelines for preparing, leading, and follow-up to a Concert of Prayer event, you'll receive a complete outline for a classic "7 Rs" Concert of Prayer that walks you minute-by-minute through a two-hour program.

This package of materials is an essential tool for pastors, youth leaders, worship leaders, Sunday School teachers, small group leaders, or anyone who wants practical, how-to suggestions on praying with others for spiritual awakening and global evangelization.

To order, use the reply form that follows, or write or call:

Concerts of Prayer International
P.O. Box 1399 • Wheaton, IL 60189
COPI office: 630-690-8441 • 24-Hour Request Line: 1-800-576-6458

Continuing Education for Church Leaders

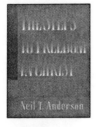

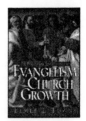

Helping Others Find Freedom in Christ

Neil T. Anderson

Help people become better connected to God with "discipleship counseling." Neil Anderson gives you clear guidelines for leading others through the steps outlined in his previous books, *Victory Over the Darkness* and *The Bondage Breaker.*

Paperback • ISBN 08307.17862

Video Training Program
• SPCN 85116.00949

The Steps to Freedom in Christ

Neil T. Anderson

This spiritual and personal inventory allows a person to help others or themselves break free from addictive and debilitating habits and beliefs.

The Steps to Freedom in Christ Guidebook • ISBN 08307.18508

Freedom from Addiction

Neil T. Anderson and Mike and Julia Quarles

Here's a Christ-centered model for recovery that has already helped thousands of people break free from alcoholism, drug addiction and other addictive behaviors.

Hardcover • ISBN 08307.17579

Evangelism and Church Growth

Elmer L. Towns

In one volume you get everything from Sunday School lesson plans to suggestions for launching a capital fund drive. Dr. Elmer Towns pulls together the most up-to-date, definitive work on evangelism and church growth available today.

Hardcover • ISBN 08307.18575

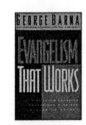

Turning Vision into Action

George Barna

George Barna lays out powerful how-to action steps to implement the vision that God has for your ministry—and how you can bring it to life both in your church and at home.

Hardcover • ISBN 08307.18524

Evangelism that Works

George Barna

Get an up-to-the-minute view of the unchurched in America, and about successful efforts to reach them. Through interviews and surveys, Barna provides feedback on methods of soul-winning that are working.

Paperback • ISBN 08307.17765

Resurrecting Hope

John Perkins with Jo Kadlecek

A dramatic profile of 10 churches that are working positively and successfully in the city. These churches provide a powerful model of hope for any ministry.

Hardcover • ISBN 08307.17757

Healing America's Wounds

John Dawson

This reconciler's handbook provides a way to deal with sexual conflict, political polarization, divisive Christians, racial tension and more.

Paperback • ISBN 08307.16939

Ask for these resources at your local Christian bookstore.

Resources for Cutting Edge Leaders

Setting Your Church Free

Neil T. Anderson and Charles Mylander

Spiritual battles can affect entire churches as well as individuals. *Setting Your Church Free* shows pastors and church leaders how they can apply the powerful principles from *Victory Over the Darkness* to lead their churches to freedom.

Hardcover • ISBN 08307.16556

What the Bible Says About Healthy Living

Rex Russell, M.D.

Learn three biblical principles that will help you improve your physical—and spiritual—health. This book gives you practical, workable steps to improve your health and overall quality of life.

Paperback • ISBN 08307.18583

The Healthy Church

C. Peter Wagner

When striving for health and growth of a church, we often overlook things that are killing us. If we can detect and counteract these diseases we can grow a healthy, Christ-directed church.

Hardcover • ISBN 08307.18346

Fasting for Spiritual Breakthrough

Elmer L. Towns

This book gives you the biblical reasons for fasting, and introduces you to nine biblical fasts—each designed for a specific physical and spiritual outcome.

Paperback • ISBN 08307.18397

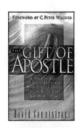

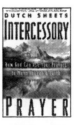

The Voice of God

Cindy Jacobs

Cut through confusion and see how prophecy can be used in any church. You'll get a clear picture of biblical prophecy and how an individual can exercise this spiritual gift to edify the church.

Paperback • ISBN 08307.17730

The Gift of Apostle

David Cannistraci

Find out why God has given the Church apostles—leaders with a clear mission to mobilize and unify the church—and see what the Bible says about the apostolic gift for today's church.

Hardcover • ISBN 08307.18451

Intercessory Prayer

Dutch Sheets

Find inspiration to reach new levels of prayer, the courage to pray for the "impossible" and the persistence to see your prayers through to completion.

"Of all the books on prayer I have read, none compares to Intercessory Prayer!" –C. Peter Wagner

Hardcover • ISBN 08307.18885

That None Should Perish

Ed Silvoso

Ed Silvoso shows that dramatic things happen when we pray for people. Learn the powerful principles of "prayer evangelism" and how to bring the gospel to your community, reaching your entire city for Christ.

Paperback • ISBN 08307.16904

Ask for these resources at your local Christian bookstore.

Regal
A Division of Gospel Light

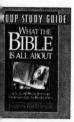